BAFFINS
BAY

ARCTIC LAND

DA

Hudsons Charles Straits

NEW NORTH
WALES

TERRA
LABRADOR

NEW SOUTH
WALES

HUDSONS BAY

NEW
BRITAIN

WALES

L. PISCOUTAGAMI

L. TABITTIBIS
MISION

NEW FRANCE

LAKE SUPERIOR

50

The Main
Bank

Falls
Bank

40

LAKE
HURON

LAKE
ERIE

PENN

MARY
LAND

VIRGI
NIA

CAROLINA

Cape Cod

Bermudes alt
Summer Iland

30

SEA OF THE ENGLISH EMPIRE

Part of Land
of Wild Bulls

THE GOLF or
BAY OF
MEXICO

BAHAMA
ISLANDS

ANTILLES Is

WEST INDIAN

20

SEA
CARIBY
ISLANDS

YUCATAN

10

HONDRAS

VENE

MARTA

PARIA
NEX

MANDALUSIA

· VOICES ·
from
COLONIAL AMERICA

FLORIDA

1513–1821

MATTHEW C. CANNAVALE

WITH

ROBERT OLWELL, PH.D., CONSULTANT

NATIONAL GEOGRAPHIC
WASHINGTON, D.C.

One of the world's largest nonprofit scientific and educational organizations, the National Geographic Society was founded in 1888 "for the increase and diffusion of geographic knowledge." Fulfilling this mission, the Society educates and inspires millions every day through its magazine, books, television programs, videos, maps and atlases, research grants, the National Geographic Bee, teacher workshops, and innovative classroom materials. The Society is supported through membership dues, charitable gifts, and income from the sale of its educational products. This support is vital to National Geographic's mission to increase global understanding and promote conservation of our planet through exploration, research, and education.

For more information, please call 1-800-NGS LINE (647-5463) or write to the following address:

NATIONAL GEOGRAPHIC SOCIETY
1145 17th Street N.W.
Washington, D.C. 20036-4688
U.S.A.

Visit the Society's Web site at www.nationalgeographic.com.

John M. Fahey, Jr., *President and Chief Executive Officer*
Gilbert M. Grosvenor, *Chairman of the Board*
Nina D. Hoffman, *Executive Vice President, President Book Publishing Group*

STAFF FOR THIS BOOK

Nancy Laties Feresten, *Vice President, Editor-in-Chief of Children's Books*
Suzanne Patrick Fonda, *Project Editor*
Robert D. Johnston, Ph.D., *Associate Professor and Director, Teaching of History Program University of Illinois at Chicago, Series Editor*
Bea Jackson, *Director of Illustration and Design, Children's Books*
Jean Cantu, *Illustrations Specialist*
Carl Mehler, *Director of Maps*
Justin Morrill, *The M Factory, Inc., Map Research, Design, and Production*
Rebecca Baines, *Editorial Assistant*
Rebecca Hinds, *Managing Editor*
Margie Towery, *Indexer*
R. Gary Colbert, *Production Director*
Lewis R. Bassford, *Production Manager*
Vincent P. Ryan and Maryclare Tracy, *Manufacturing Managers*

Voices from Colonial Florida was prepared by
CREATIVE MEDIA APPLICATIONS, INC.
Matthew C. Cannavale, *Writer*
Fabia Wargin Design, Inc., *Design and Production*
Susan Madoff, *Editor*
Laurie Lieb, *Copyeditor*
Jennifer Bright, *Image Researcher*

Body text is set in Deepdene, sidebars are Caslon 337 Oldstyle, and display text is Cochin Archaic Bold.

LIBRARY OF CONGRESS CATALOGING-IN-PUBLICATION DATA
Cannavale, Matthew C.
   Voices from colonial America. Florida 1513–1821 / by Matthew C. Cannavale.
      p. cm. — (Voices from colonial America)
   Includes bibliographical references and index.
   ISBN-10: 0-7922-6409-6 (Hardcover)
   ISBN-13: 978-0-7922-6409-5 (Hardcover)
   ISBN-10: 0-7922-6866-0 (Library)
   ISBN-13: 978-0-7922-6866-6 (Library)
   1. Florida—History—To 1821—Juvenile literature. I. National Geographic Society (U.S.) II. Title. III. Title: Florida 1513–1821.
   F314.C1955 2006
   975.9'01—dc22
                                        2006020505

Printed in Belgium

CONTENTS

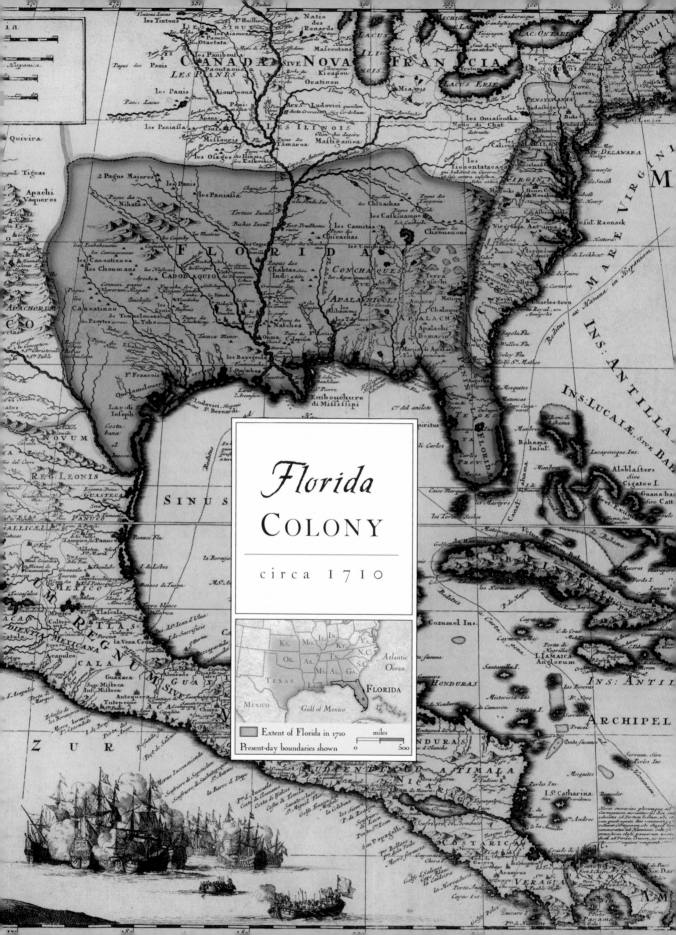

Florida

COLONY

circa 1710

Extent of Florida in 1710
Present-day boundaries shown

miles
0   500

INTRODUCTION

by

Robert Olwell, Ph.D.

One of Florida's largest cotton plantations, the Kingsley Plantation,
located in what is now Jacksonville, was owned by Zephaniah Kingsley.
When he died, it became the property of his wife,
Anna Majigeen Jai Kingsley, a freed slave.

From Ponce de León's first landfall in 1513 to its acquisition
by the United States in 1821, Florida's colonial history spans
more than four centuries. Yet, despite its remarkable
longevity, colonial Florida was a delicate and shallow rooted
"flower," constantly buffeted by the winds of rival empires.
Always menaced with attack from without and lacking the

OPPOSITE: The green area on this historical map shows the area that
Spain claimed as its Florida Colony in 1710. The inset map shows the
present-day states that were once part of this colony.

Native Americans in Florida in the mid-1500s
gather around a fire. The fortified village in
this colored engraving published in 1591
shows wigwams where the Indians lived,
structures used for crop storage, and
a stockade fence surrounding the village
to protect the residents from attacks by
hostile tribes.

natural resources (such as gold and silver) that would have repaid a large investment of men and materials, the Florida colony was for most of its history merely a pawn used to protect more valuable colonial possessions elsewhere.

Colonial Florida inspired dreamers such as Juan Ponce de León, Pánfilo de Narváez and Hernando de Soto. They came to Florida with visions of kingdoms of gold to conquer and plunder. In 1562, French Protestants (Huguenots) came to Florida to found a colony where they could live free of religious persecution. Spanish missionaries arrived soon after with high expectations of making Catholics of Indians (some 20,000 would eventually be baptized). Some Indians, like the Creeks, dreamed of revenge against their Spanish enemy, and the English aspired to imperial glory and personal wealth.

As the British colonies to the north grew and prospered, Indians driven out of the Southeast by British settlers, and African slaves escaping from British-born masters were given refuge and freedom by the Spanish. But by the mid-

18th century Spanish Florida served little purpose beyond being a thorn in the side of the British lion. British diplomats removed the thorn when they traded Cuba (which Britain had captured from Spain) for Florida in 1763. But, in 1783, when the British acknowledged the independence of the newly proclaimed United States, they also returned Florida to Spain.

By the end of the 18th century, the Spanish Empire was in decline throughout the Western Hemisphere. Spain could do little to police Florida's frontiers. Faced with threats to take the region by force, Spain at last agreed to sell Florida to the United States. When the Stars and Stripes were finally raised above the Castillo de San Marcos in Saint Augustine in 1821, Florida's long colonial history came to an end.

In *Voices from Colonial America: Florida*, readers will discover that beyond the narrow streets of old Saint Augustine, modern Florida retains little trace of its colonial heritage. Names that dot the state are one link to the colonial era. The Saint Johns (San Juan) River, Matanzas Inlet, and Cape Canaveral were christened by the Spanish. Lake George, New Smyrna, Halifax River, and Egmont Key (at the entrance to Tampa Bay) were all named when Florida was a British colony. Likewise, historic markers and archaeological excavations provide evidence of an era when Florida was inhabited by proud Indians, resolute Africans, and ambitious Europeans. Like their colonial ancestors, modern Floridians continue to dream that the future will be greater than the past.

CHAPTER ONE

The Conquistadors

1513 — 1559

JUAN PONCE DE LEÓN claims Florida for Spain in 1513. More than forty years of Spanish exploration follows, but a thriving Spanish colony in Florida remains out of reach.

On the morning of Sunday, April 3, 1513, land was spotted to the port side of a ship sailing in the Atlantic. On board, Juan Ponce de León, a Spanish military leader and explorer, prepared to go ashore to take possession of the newly sighted land for Spain.

Slave traders in Puerto Rico, where Ponce de León had a plantation, had spoken of a large island to the north where they had captured Indians to sell as slaves in the Spanish

OPPOSITE: Juan Ponce de León, spurred on by the desire to find the Fountain of Youth, claimed Florida for Spain in 1513. His discovery prompted the Spanish to continue exploring the region for the next 50 years.

colonies in the Caribbean. In early March of 1513, de León had ventured north from San Juan, Puerto Rico, with three ships, the *Santiago*, the *Santa Maria de la Consolacion*, and the *San Cristobal*. With him was a force of about 65 people, including sailors, soldiers, Indian slaves, and Africans.

De León and a small group of men went ashore somewhere north of what is today Daytona Beach in Florida. They planted a cross in the sand, claiming the land in the name of King Ferdinand of Spain. De León believed he had discovered a large island. He named it *la Florida* (the flowered one) to honor Pascua Florida, meaning "Feast of Flowers," the Spanish Easter celebration, and because the area was full of trees beginning to blossom. He explored the area briefly to find fresh water and search for signs of

THE RISE OF SPAIN

and the

Conquistadors

IN 1492 SPAIN ENDED MORE than 700 years of warfare by defeating the Moors, an Islamic people from northern Africa who had invaded Spain in A.D. 711. The years of fighting had strengthened the Spanish Army and Navy. Spain now looked to expand its empire. Through the battles with the Moors, many young soldiers had proven themselves. They now turned their sights to the exploration of new lands and the riches and glory they hoped to find. These soldiers became the conquistadors, who conquered lands near and far for the honor of the Spanish crown.

native people. Finding none, he returned to his ship and set sail to the south, following the coast.

Along the way, de León and his men noticed several groups of natives on the shore. De León decided to go ashore with a group of men in small boats. Antonio de Herrera y Tordesillias, a 16th-century historian, described this first meeting between de León and the Native Americans:

> De León went ashore here [probably near present-day Daytona Beach and] was called by the Indians who, in turn tried to take the small boat, the oars, and arms. Because he did not want to start a fight he had to tolerate their taunts. . . . Because the Indians hit a sailor in the head with a stick knocking him unconscious, he [de León] had to fight with them.

JUAN PONCE DE LEÓN & THE FOUNTAIN OF YOUTH

ACCORDING TO A POPULAR MYTH, the Fountain of Youth, a magical spring that flowed with rejuvenating waters, was located on one of the islands north of San Juan, Puerto Rico. Peter Martyr, a famous historian living during de León's time, wrote: *Among the islands of the north side of Hispaniola, there is an Island about 325 leagues [975 miles] distant . . . in which is a continual spring of water, of such marvelous virtue that the water thereof being drunk . . . maketh old men young again.* De León was 56 years old when he set out to explore the islands north of Puerto Rico. Though he never left any official mention of the Fountain of Youth, it remains possible that he hoped to find its magic waters.

Three Indians using dried deer skins for camouflage approach a river, their bows ready to shoot the deer standing on the opposite bank.

The Indians attacked the party with spears and arrows made of sharpened bone, injuring two of de León's men. The Spaniards fought back with steel swords and guns and were able to escape. De León took one Indian prisoner with the hope of teaching him Spanish and using him as a guide. These natives were most likely Timucua Indians.

After the encounter with the Timucua, de León had his ships sail around the tip of Florida and back up the western coast. On June 4, 1513, de León and his three ships entered what is today Charlotte Harbor.

While they were anchored there, de León and his men defended themselves from attacks by another group of natives. One Indian captured during the attack spoke some Spanish, proving that slave traders had been there earlier. Rather than continue to engage in battle, de León left Charlotte Harbor and set sail for San Juan.

CALUSA

UNKNOWN TO DE LEÓN, HE HAD STUMBLED UPON A LARGE and advanced civilization. The Calusa were a dominant native group in southern Florida at that time whose civilization could be traced back more than 12,000 years. Like the Timucua to the north, the Calusa were fierce warriors. They gained a reputation for capturing and enslaving or sacrificing European sailors and explorers.

The Calusa constructed some of their towns on mounds of seashells. Their largest town was a fortress built near present-day Estero Bay. The fortress was built on an artificial island built from shells piled up from the bottom of the bay.

The Calusa were skilled fishermen and accomplished sailors. They harvested huge quantities of shellfish and navigated their 15-foot (4.6-m) wooden canoes as far as Cuba and the Bahamas.

De León wanted to return to Florida, but it was seven years before he was able. In early 1521, de León wrote: "I discovered Florida and some other small islands at my own expense, and now I am going to settle them with plenty of men and two ships, and I am going to explore the coast, to see if it compares with (other) lands."

On February 20, 1521, de León set sail with two ships, nearly one hundred people, and the seed, animals, and other materials needed to establish a colony. In mid-March, de León and his ships landed near what is today

Fort Myers, south of Charlotte Harbor. De León chose the location because of its natural harbor. He began building fortifications and housing and explored the surrounding area to locate good land for crops and sources of fresh water. In early June, the colonists were attacked by a large Calusa force who immediately overran the Spaniards. De León was shot in the leg with an arrow, and many of his men were injured or killed.

Those who were able retreated to the ships. One ship, carrying de León and the other wounded, departed for Havana, Cuba, the nearest Spanish colony. The other ship, carrying most of the survivors, headed to New Spain (Mexico) to join other expeditions. De León's wound proved fatal, and he died shortly after arriving in Havana.

PÁNFILO DE NARVÁEZ'S DOOMED EXPEDITION

At about the same time as de León's failed attempt at colonization, much of Spain's attention shifted to New Spain. Hernán Cortéz had conquered the native people and had found gold and silver there. While many conquistadors headed south, several continued the work de León had begun in Florida. They hoped to find riches like those found in New Spain.

In 1526, Pánfilo de Narváez, a veteran of many battles against Indians of the Caribbean, was given control of Florida by the Spanish crown. He was instructed to establish two towns and three forts in Florida. He departed from Spain on June 17, 1527, with 600 men and five ships. When he stopped in Santo Domingo, more than 150 of his men deserted, many to join expeditions into New Spain.

As his remaining force departed, his ships were hit by a hurricane. Two were lost along with 60 men. Narváez returned to Cuba for repairs and to restock supplies. He set sail again in February 1528. On April 14, his ship landed near present-day Tampa Bay, more than 100 miles (161 km) north of de León's failed colony. Narváez chose this location in an attempt to avoid the Calusa who had doomed de León's attempt at colonization.

Narváez split his expedition into two groups. The first, which he led, explored the inland areas by foot. The second group was to sail along the coast and meet up with their fellow explorers north of Tampa Bay. Álvar Núñez Cabeza de Vaca, Narváez's second in command, disagreed with the decision. He wrote in his journal:

> It seemed to me in no manner advisable to forsake the ships. I told him [Narváez] we had no interpreter to make ourselves understood by the natives. . . . Neither did we know what to expect from the land we were entering, having no knowledge of what it was . . . [and] finally, that we had not the supplies required for penetrating into an unknown country . . . so that, in my opinion, we should re-embark and sail in quest of a land and harbor better adapted to settlement.

Narváez's plan failed. The ships were unable to find Narváez and his men. After sailing up and down the coast for several months, they gave up and headed to New Spain.

Narváez and his party, hopelessly lost and cut off from supplies, suffered many attacks from Indians. Finally he decided to build several rafts, hoping they could locate a Spanish outpost by sailing along the coast toward New Spain. About 250 men set sail, but only de Vaca and 50 others survived the voyage, which took them to present-day Galveston, Texas. Narváez was among those who died.

HERNANDO DE SOTO EXPLORES FLORIDA

In April 1537, Hernando de Soto was given a patent to explore and colonize Florida. De Soto left Spain in 1538 with ten ships, more than 600 men, and 200 horses. After stopping in Santo Domingo

patent—a document giving official permission to explore or settle an area

and Havana to pick up additional men, he finally landed somewhere near present-day Tampa Bay in May 1539 with a force of nearly 1,000.

The need to find enough food for his men and horses brought him in contact with many groups of Indians. Though he did not count the number of Indians he met, his almost daily sightings suggest that the area was densely populated by many tribes. He was able to trade with some of the Indians. When trading did not work, he took what he needed by force, leaving a bloody trail behind him.

By October 1539, de Soto's expedition reached central Florida, near present-day Tallahassee. At the time, the area was a heavily populated Apalachee village called Anhaica, with more than 250 buildings. Apalachee scouts warned of de Soto's approach and his treatment of other Indians. Afraid of the invaders, the Apalachee abandoned their village. The Spanish camped there through the winter and departed in March 1540. De Soto crossed much of what is today the southeastern United States, including Georgia, the Carolinas, Tennessee, Alabama, Mississippi, Arkansas, Louisiana, and Texas. He was convinced he would find civilizations similar to those of Mexico, rich with gold, silver, and jewels. In 1540, he led his men south toward the Gulf of Mexico. He hoped to meet up with his ships and get additional food,

Hernando de Soto is pictured here in about 1540 at the head of the large expedition he led to explore the Florida region in search of gold.

horses, weapons, and other supplies. But he was ambushed by a large native force just under 100 miles (161 km) from his ships. Although he was able to turn back the Indians, some of his men were injured or killed. Fearing that his men would refuse to continue if they reached the ship, he moved to the north, away from the gulf.

In 1541, de Soto's expedition reached a large river that would come to be known as the Mississippi. Shortly afterward, their supplies began to run short. De Soto fell ill with a fever and died in June 1542. His troops deserted, many heading to Spanish settlements in New Spain.

MISSIONARIES ARRIVE IN FLORIDA

After de Soto's death, the Spanish crown rejected many bids by other conquistadors to colonize Florida. Deciding to try a new tactic, Spain sent missionaries instead.

missionaries— people who work to spread a religion and convert others to it

In 1549, Father Luis Cancer de Barbastro, a friar, led a small expedition to spread Christianity to the Native Americans of Florida. He hoped to seek out a friendly tribe and convert its members to Catholicism. The captain sailing Barbastro's ship anchored at Tampa Bay. On the second day, several Calusa were sighted along the shore. Unable to convince the captain to move the ship closer to shore or allow him the use of one of the ship's rowboats, Barbastro jumped overboard and swam to shore. When he reached land, he was attacked and killed while kneeling in prayer.

friar—a monk who owns no property

THE FAILED COLONY OF TRISTÁN DE LUNA

In 1559, Tristán de Luna, a conquistador, set out to establish a chain of colonies across Florida's Gulf Coast. De Luna landed near present-day Pensacola Harbor with 500 soldiers and 1,000 settlers. He sent out small groups to set up settlements outside the harbor area.

When de Soto and Narváez had passed through this area years before, they had encountered many Indians, but de Luna found few. Diseases carried by the Spanish had wiped out more than half of the area's native population.

Disaster struck when a hurricane hit Pensacola and destroyed most of de Luna's food and supplies. Hungry and ill and with his men doubting his ability to lead, he left Pensacola Bay for Mexico City, the capital of Spain's North American empire.

By now, Spain had made many unsuccessful attempts to settle Florida. The land itself offered few known resources, but its position along the Gulf Stream made it a very important strategic location for protecting the shipments of precious metals and slaves between New Spain, the Caribbean, and Europe. Even without successful colonies or useful resources, this strategic value was reason enough to keep a watchful eye on the territory. Unknown to the Spanish, however, French settlers both in Europe and in present-day Canada were making their own plans to explore the region.

CHAPTER TWO

The French in Florida

1562 — 1568

Frenchmen Jean Ribault and René de Laudonnière attempt to settle Florida, and a series of bloody massacres between French and Spanish forces take place.

n early May 1562, Jean Ribault, a French explorer, sighted an inlet near present-day Jacksonville, Florida. He and several men rowed ashore, said a prayer, and then claimed this land for the French king just as de León and others had done for the Spanish king years earlier. In the eyes of the Spanish,

OPPOSITE: French settlers at Fort Caroline can be seen in boats on the St. Johns River and working along its shores. In the foreground, Native Americans gather to watch the activity.

the French were intruding on their land. To make matters worse, Ribault was Protestant, and Protestantism was a religion that the Spanish had recently vowed to eliminate.

JEAN RIBAULT AND THE HUGUENOT COLONY

Ribault had left France in February 1562 with two ships and nearly 150 men. His expedition would serve two purposes: finding a location for a Huguenot colony and testing how the Spanish would respond to rival exploration.

Huguenot—a French Protestant

After going ashore and claiming the land for France, Ribault ordered his men to construct a stone pillar to mark the French land claim. Ribault and his crew then returned to their ship and sailed north in search of a good harbor and a location for an outpost. They came to a small island off the coast of present-day South Carolina. Ribault described the island as *"one of the greatest and fairest havens of the world."* He was so impressed with the land that he built a small fort named Charlesfort, to honor King Charles of France, and left 26 of his men behind to occupy it.

Ribault planned to return to France, collect supplies, and depart once again for his colony. But when he arrived in France, he found the country torn by war between the French Catholics and the Huguenots. When he traveled to

England to ask for help with his colony, he was imprisoned for his religious beliefs.

When Ribault did not return, those who remained at Charlesfort began to worry. They built a ship to sail back to France. The ship was poorly constructed and did not have enough food and water supplies. During the voyage home, many men died of disease. When the food ran out, they tried to eat their boots and other goods made of leather. Eventually they killed a man and ate him. Only seven of the original 26 survived the voyage home.

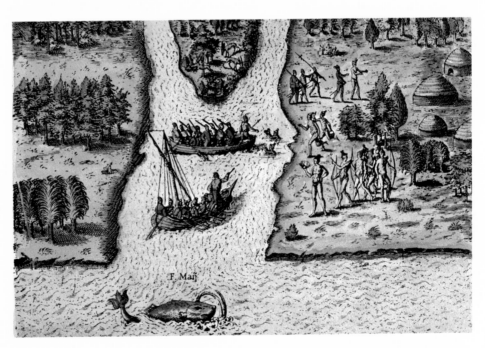

A 1591 engraving by Johann Théodor de Bry shows French ships in the River of May (the present-day St. Johns River) greeting Native Americans living in the area. Fort Caroline would be built in this strategic spot where the French could capture and rob Spanish ships sailing from South America, heavy with silver and gold.

In this engraving based on a drawing by French explorer
Jacques Le Moyne de Morgues, René de Laudonnière (right) stands with
Timucua chief Athore in front of the stone pillar that Jean Ribault had
erected when he claimed the land for France in 1562.

RENÉ DE LAUDONNIÈRE
TAKES COMMAND

René de Laudonnière had been second in command on
Ribault's first voyage. With Ribault imprisoned in
England, Laudonnière was asked to lead a large colonization attempt in Florida. King Charles IX gave him three
ships, and Laudonnière recruited soldiers as well as people
who wanted to settle the region. The colonists included
young and old, male and female, rich and poor, Protestants
and Catholics.

Laudonnière departed France in early 1564 with 304 soldiers and more than 200 colonists. Unsure of the condition Charlesfort had been left in, he guided his ships to the original site where Ribault had constructed the stone pillar. They landed on June 22. The soldiers and colonists worked together to construct a fort and other buildings for the colony, which Laudonnière named Fort Caroline. They explored the surrounding area and formed a peaceful relationship with the Timucua Indians who lived there.

Work was difficult, however, and settlers began to complain. Laudonnière feared he would lose control of the colony, so he selected the colonists he thought most likely to oppose him and sent them back to France on one of his ships. Morale improved for a little while, but then others began to challenge his leadership, so he sent them on missions to explore the surrounding areas. Most of these

PICTURING
the New World

ONE OF THE COLONISTS WHO traveled with Laudonnière was an artist named Jacques Le Moyne de Morgues. At Fort Caroline, he made many drawings of the animals and plants of the surrounding area. He also painted portraits of the Timucua and their villages. All but one of his works were destroyed before he returned to France. Once home, he re-created many of them based on notes and memory. He planned to use them to illustrate a book about his adventures in the New World, but he died before finishing the project. An artist and editor named Johann Théodor de Bry purchased his works and notes and used them to write and illustrate a book about the adventures of Laudonnière and Ribault. De Bry's book contains what are considered some of the oldest and most accurate images of the New World.

groups did not return, choosing instead to desert inland or to the south. Many of the deserters began raiding Timucua villages, causing the Indians to quickly withdraw their support for the remaining colonists.

Laudonnière feared he did not have enough people to build a lasting colony, so in early August 1565, he began plans to abandon Fort Caroline and return to France. Meanwhile, in England, Jean Ribault had been released from prison. Upon his return to France, he spoke with King Charles IX, who feared that Laudonnière had lost control of the colony at Fort Caroline. The king made plans to send Ribault and 500 soldiers to reinforce the colony and restore order.

MENÉNDEZ DRIVES THE FRENCH FROM FLORIDA

Reports of the French colony and Ribault's intention to reinforce it spread. These reports angered Philip II of Spain. He saw Fort Caroline as a direct challenge to Spanish control in Florida and the Caribbean, an insult to his defense of the Catholic Church, and a threat to the gold and silver shipments from New Spain that ran along the Florida coast. A French colony would threaten Spanish access to the Gulf Stream, which had become essential in speeding gold and silver from the New World back to Spain.

Philip II sent Pedro Menéndez de Avilés, an experienced naval officer, and a force of 2,000 soldiers to remove the French settlers from Spanish Florida. In return for his services, Menéndez was made *Adelantado*, or military governor, of Florida.

Pedro Menéndez de Avilés,
Adelantado of Florida

In spring 1565, Ribault left France with seven ships and 500 soldiers. Menéndez left Spain with eleven ships. He hoped to reach Fort Caroline first, easily take the fort, and surprise Ribault and his men when they arrived. Menéndez's ships raced across the Atlantic and reached the Florida coast on August 28. They followed the coast north and sighted Ribault's ships, which had arrived only days before. Menéndez knew that Ribault's ships were faster and had better cannon. Rather than attack the French ships, Menéndez sailed south in search of a safe harbor.

Menéndez followed the coast about 30 miles (48 km), and on September 8, found a natural harbor near Anastasia Island. There, he unloaded his men and their weapons and supplies. He declared the area the site of the town of Saint Augustine. Expecting an attack by the French, he sent his ships south and prepared to defend the land.

Ribault sent out scouts, who reported Menéndez's position. Ribault knew that his best chance to defeat the Spanish would be to attack before they reinforced their position. Rather than march his men along the coast, Ribault decided to load them into ships and sail south to attack from the sea. Laudonnière remained at Fort Caroline with a small garrison of women, children, and sick or wounded men.

garrison—troops stationed at a military outpost

On September 8, only hours after Menéndez's ships left Saint Augustine, Ribault's were spotted on the horizon. But disaster struck Ribault's force when a hurricane blew his ships south, past Saint Augustine, and smashed them on the coast. Having watched Ribault's ships sail past his camp and realizing it would be difficult for them to return until after the storm, Menéndez gathered his men and marched nearly 40 miles (64 km) north through the hurricane to Fort Caroline. His men marched through torrential rains and swamp water that was at times chest-deep. Reaching the fort before dawn on September 20, Menéndez attacked.

torrential—rapid, heavy flow

Laudonnière and many of his men were sleeping when the attack began. They awoke to the shouts of battle. He had few soldiers who could defend the fort, which was quickly overrun by the Spanish. Most of the French forces at Fort Caroline were killed. Some, including Laudonnière and Jacques Le Moyne de Morgues, escaped and hid in the wilderness. Others were captured and later hanged. Menéndez had signs placed above the dead bodies that read: *"I do this not as to Frenchmen, but as to Lutherans [Protestants]."*

Pedro Menéndez de Avilés (seated) surveys the Spanish surprise attack on the French at Fort Caroline. The soldiers waiting to speak with him are probably informing their commander of an imminent victory over the French.

After the battle, Menéndez renamed the fort San Mateo. Leaving some of his troops to guard the fort, he returned with the rest of his men to Saint Augustine, still expecting Ribault's force to return and attack. Several days later, scouts reported that Ribault's men were stranded on the beach along a river south of Saint Augustine. Menéndez headed south with nearly 50 men. He found almost 500 French, many injured, tired, and hungry. Menéndez knew he could not feed or guard so many prisoners. Instead, he chose to execute most of them, killing 334, including Ribault. The river is known today as Matanzas, from the Spanish word for "massacre." News of the massacre eventually reached France, but King Charles IX decided not to retaliate.

The French did not give up exploring North America altogether. Instead, they focused their efforts far north of the Spanish forces in Florida.

retaliate—to take revenge

To protect the Spanish position, Menéndez ordered San Mateo fortified and several smaller outposts built along the coast between San Mateo and Saint Augustine. He ordered the construction of a town and fort at Saint Augustine and then went to Spain to request additional troops and supplies.

THE FRENCH RESPONSE

News spread of the French massacre and the French government's decision not to retaliate. Many French were upset, but could do little to fight back against Spain. Dominique de Gourgues, a French soldier, trader, sailor, and, by many accounts, pirate, decided to take matters into his own hands.

De Gourgues knew that the French government would not approve a private attack on the Spanish troops in Florida. Instead he told everyone he was sailing to Africa to capture slaves and then sell them in the Caribbean. He secured three ships, 150 soldiers, and 80 sailors with his own savings and began his mission in August 1567. After capturing slaves, he sailed to Hispaniola, where he sold his cargo. Setting sail from Hispaniola, he headed north toward the Gulf Stream, which would carry his ships back to Europe. But en route, he called his men together and explained his true plan.

He retold the story of the Spanish massacre of the French troops and then asked, *"Shall we let such cruelty go unpunished? What fame for us if we avenge it! To this end I have given my fortune, and I counted on you to help me. Was I wrong?"* He said that he planned to attack the Spanish troops at San Mateo, and his men agreed to support him.

He and his men went ashore north of the fort. They were met by Timucua Indians who recognized their clothing and realized they were not Spanish. Though relations between the French and the Timucua were not good, relations between the Spanish and the Indians were much worse. De Gourgues met with the Timucua chief Satouriona, the old friend of Laudonnière, and through a translator they agreed to attack the Spanish together.

Satouriona called together an army of several hundred Timucua warriors. Along with de Gourgues's troops, they greatly outnumbered the Spanish forces at San Mateo and the two small outposts that Menéndez had constructed to the south. The French and their Timucua allies first attacked

French soldiers and their Timuca allies battle another tribe in the region in this 1591 colored engraving by Théodor de Bry.

the outposts, each housing fewer than 60 Spanish defenders. Few were taken prisoner; most were killed.

Early the next morning the French and Timucua force attacked San Mateo. The Spanish were terrified. Many tried to escape into the forest, but the Timucua warriors hunted them down and killed them. Few survived, and most of those who did were captured and then hanged at the same place Menéndez had hanged the French prisoners three years earlier. According to some accounts, De Gourgues had signs placed above the hanged bodies that read: *"I do this not as to Spaniards, but as to Traitors, Robbers, and Murderers."*

Sir Francis Drake Attacks Saint Augustine

Saint Augustine was growing into an important Spanish military outpost. It was the center of the Florida colony and home to 300 soldiers and their families. A wooden fort had been constructed on the outskirts of the city as well as a series of watchtowers.

In 1585, war broke out between England and Spain in Europe. Spain used much of the gold and silver from the New World to pay for its war. The English realized that the best way to defeat Spain was to attack the silver and gold shipments coming from the New World.

Sir Francis Drake was an English privateer. He sailed to the Caribbean with a fleet of 23 ships and more than 2,000 men with an order to attack and loot Spanish ships, ports, and cities. On May 28, 1586,

privateer—captain of a private ship, armed and hired to attack ships from another country

Drake sailed into Saint Augustine harbor. His ships bombarded the city. During the night, most of the Spanish abandoned the fort and the city. In the morning, Drake and more than 1,000 soldiers came ashore and stormed the city. Nearly every Spaniard who remained in Saint Augustine was killed. Drake collected supplies, food, and anything else useful from the town. Then his men burned it to the ground.

After Drake left, the Spanish who had fled returned to the city and began rebuilding. Menéndez realized that a wooden fortress would not be enough to protect the city or the ships that sailed up the coast. He wrote to Spain asking for money and supplies to build a stone fort at Saint Augustine. His request was denied. Spain was more concerned with battles in Europe and control of colonies in the Caribbean and South America than in protecting Saint Augustine. ✳

The Spanish Mission Period

1567 — 1670

JESUITS AND, LATER, FRANCISCAN MISSIONARIES *travel to Florida to "civilize" the natives and build a series of missions that provide food for the soldiers at Saint Augustine.*

 preading the Catholic religion had long been a goal of the Spanish. Official patents for exploring and colonizing Florida often stated, *"our principal intent in the discovery of new lands is that the inhabitants and natives thereof, who are without the light or knowledge of faith, may be brought to understand the truth of our holy Catholic Faith."*

OPPOSITE: By the early 1600s, the settlement at Saint Augustine had been rebuilt according to a plan laid out by the governor. Palm trees dotted the narrow streets, and houses with balconies echoed architecture found in Spain.

But such religious goals had often been secondary to protecting the silver and gold fleets that sailed the Gulf Stream along Florida's eastern coast.

Menéndez and many others of his time believed that converting Native Americans to Catholicism was the first step to "civilizing" them. He believed that civilized

converting—convincing people to change their beliefs

Indians would be less of a threat to the Spanish and a source of labor for the Spanish forts. Menéndez asked King Philip II to send more priests to serve as missionaries.

Shortly after the establishment of Saint Augustine, Philip sent three Jesuit friars, Brother Pedro Martinez, Brother Juan Rogel, and Brother Francisco de

Jesuit—a Catholic religious order founded by Saint Ignatius Loyola

Villareal, to Florida. They landed in Saint Augustine. From there, a small party of soldiers and sailors led by Brother Martinez, an experienced missionary, sailed north. They reached what is today Cumberland Island off the coast of southern Georgia. Most of the party went ashore, but a few sailors remained on the ship. After several nights on the island, the group was attacked and killed by Indians. The remaining sailors aboard the ship fled to Saint Augustine to relay what had happened.

Hearing of Brother Martinez's death, Brothers Rogel and Villareal decided to stay close to Saint Augustine and study the Indians of the area and their language. The Jesuits worked with different groups of Indians with different cultures and languages. The missionaries also translated the Bible into the languages of the various Indian tribes. With basic knowledge of Indian languages and translations of the Bible, the Jesuits pushed north and west.

Although the Jesuits visited a great number of Indians, they did not convert many to Catholicism. They decided to withdraw from Florida and focus on work in New Spain, where they were much more successful. The work of the missionaries in Florida was

A Jesuit priest preaches to Native Americans gathered around a campfire inside a primitive structure.

Franciscan—a Catholic religious order founded by Saint Francis of Assisi

abandoned until 1573, when the Franciscans, another Catholic order, offered to continue the work started by the Jesuits.

FRANCISCAN MISSIONARIES

In 1577, Father Alonso de Reynoso, a Franciscan priest and missionary, traveled to Saint Augustine. He began working with members of the tribes near the town. Within a short time, Indians from two nearby villages were attending church services in Saint Augustine. Over the years that followed, additional Franciscan missionaries were sent to Florida. In 1587 formal missions called *doctrinas* were built in each of the two Indian villages outside of Saint Augustine. Once the doctrinas were completed, Indians attended church service in their own villages with the assistance of priests from Saint Augustine. Doctrinas were built from logs as large, square structures that differed from the usually round huts most Florida Indians lived in. The doctrinas included a chapel and a convent, which were used only for events related to religious matters. When Spanish traders or officials visited a village with a doctrina, they met with the chief in either the chief's home or a large hall. Missionaries controlled only religious activities, while chiefs maintained control of all other activities in the village.

doctrina—a small mission set up in Indian villages which included a building for religious services and a building for missionaries to live in

convent—living quarters for a monk or nun

The Franciscan missions quickly spread along the Florida coast. By 1593 there were more than 20 missionaries at work in villages of the Timucua and Yamassee Indians. The Franciscans were more successful than the Jesuits for several reasons. One of the most important was timing. When the Jesuits were working with various tribes, the natives had limited and usually negative contact with the Spanish. Attacks by conquistadors and kidnappings by slave traders were still fresh in their minds. Jesuit missionaries had to work hard to show that they were not going to harm the Indians. By the time the Franciscans reached the Florida Indians, many of the tribes had become used to interacting with the Spanish.

The Franciscans also used a different approach than the Jesuits to convert the Indians. Rather than learning tribal languages and cultures, they gave gifts such as Spanish clothes and trinkets to the chiefs and other important members of the tribe. To thank the Franciscans, chiefs often allowed a doctrina to be built in their village. Once a doctrina was built, the village could receive a missionary to be stationed there. Otherwise, the Indians had to travel to the nearest village with a doctrina for religious teaching.

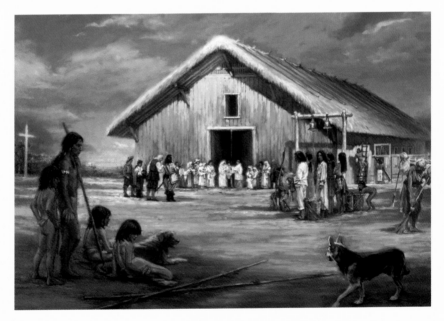

Apalachee Indians attend religious services at the Franciscan church at Mission San Luis de Talimali near present-day Tallahassee.

Most Indian groups in Florida worked as communities, growing a large field of crops for the people of the village to share. They also grew crops in private fields for the chief and other important members of the village, such as a shaman or an interpreter.

shaman—a native non-Christian religious leader, witch doctor, or spirit healer

When not working to supply food, the Indians completed daily chores or repaired structures in their villages. Missionaries were pressured to persuade the Indians to work more hours in order to help the Spanish. Writing in the early 1600s, a missionary visiting an Indian village for the first time wrote, *"they are idle most of the time, women and men alike."* The missionaries began by having Indians help with small tasks at the doctrina and then required them to grow an additional private field of crops for the missionaries and the king of Spain. Crops from the king's field were sent to outposts across Florida and, later, across the Caribbean and New Spain. This payment in food and labor that helped support the mission was known as the *sabana*. Missions were also supported by *situado*, money and supplies sent from Spain.

Once Indians accepted Catholicism and gave up any tribal religion, they were baptized and made members of the Catholic Church. When they became Catholic they were no longer seen as "savages" in the eyes of the Spanish, though Indians were still treated little better than slaves in many areas. In addition to winning converts to the Catholic faith, missionaries often introduced new skills to the

Indians. They taught Indians to ride horses and care for cattle. They also shared tools such as shovels and hammers.

The Franciscans tried to change the Indian cultures and customs to match European ways. Once Indians were baptized, they were given a Spanish name. Males were required to cut their hair and keep it short. Customs and holidays that were based on religious beliefs that were not Catholic were ended.

The sabana system was gradually expanded. The arrange-

A missionary in Florida baptizes a Native American child while his converted parents look on.

ment soon included a donation of labor from each village that became known as *repartimiento*. Young Indian men were

repartimiento—free labor provided by Indian villages to Spanish towns and outposts

sent to work in the outposts or in Saint Augustine. Each Indian village was required to send a number of young men, based on the number of people living in the village, to help with construction or supply food to soldiers or colonists living there. The Indians were required to work from two to six months, but often they were forced to stay longer. At first, the donation of crops and labor was given willingly, but over time, as the demands increased, missionaries often used whips or other types of punishment on Indians who missed work. Indian girls and women were also brought to the outposts and to Saint Augustine to marry the Spanish soldiers and settlers.

THE APALACHEE

Many Apalachee chiefs far to the west of Saint Augustine were interested in trading with the Spanish and had requested missionaries to be sent to their land as early as 1607. But the Franciscans delayed. Instead of sending missionaries to remote areas, they expanded their missions in a chain extending out from Saint Augustine. Each mission was about one day's ride on horseback from the next one. A new mission was not built until the previous one was safe and running well. Therefore,

PELOTA

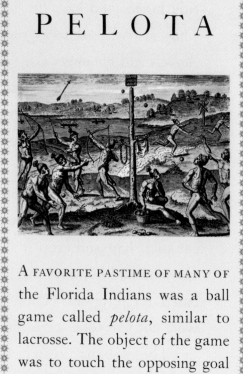

A FAVORITE PASTIME OF MANY OF the Florida Indians was a ball game called *pelota*, similar to lacrosse. The object of the game was to touch the opposing goal with a leather ball about the size of a golf ball. The goals were sticks driven into the ground at opposite ends of the playing field. The rules allowed nearly any means possible to get the ball to the goal. Some players used their speed, others their strength, and others tried to frustrate or confuse opponents. The games were often paired with celebrations and gambling.

Franciscans did not reach the Apalachee until 1633. They were well received and continued to expand the chain of missions westward all the way to what is now known as the panhandle of Florida.

Unlike the marshy areas around Saint Augustine, the lands of the Apalachee were much more fertile. The area quickly became the most important farming land in Florida, drawing some settlers from Saint Augustine. Many crops, including corn and wheat, were grown there and shipped back to Saint Augustine and then Cuba.

One of the largest and most important missions was San Luis de Apalachee, built near present-day Tallahassee. The mission was constructed in an Indian village of several hundred. But it quickly grew into a city with Spanish colonists, more than 1,400 Apalachee, and a small fort. Though Spanish and Apalachee worked side by side in San Luis, they lived in different sections of the town and in different types of houses. The Spanish built rectangular houses similar to houses of today. The Apalachee built large round houses made from a round frame of wooden posts covered with layers of leaves. Most houses were between 18 and 24 feet (5.5 and 7 m) in diameter, while the chief's house was nearly 70 feet (21 m) across. The only other major structure was the council house. It measured 120 feet (37 m) across and could seat more than 2,000 people. The council house had small rooms around the outside walls that were used by visitors and guests of the tribe. The Catholic church at San Luis was built in 1656. It was 110 feet (34 m) long and 50 feet (15 m) wide. The church contained a large altar and choir loft and was decorated with paintings and sculptures.

A representation of the Mission San Luis de Apalachee shows the fort with blockhouse (far left) and the mission's circular plaza (right). The plaza served as the site for traditional Apalachee activities and as a central marketplace. Around the plaza are the Stations of the Cross used by the Catholic priests, Spanish, and converts to remember the sufferings of Christ before his crucifixion. The large conical structure (far right) is the Apalachee Council House. Next to it is the chief's house. The two rectangular buildings are the Franciscan church (right) and friary where the missionaries lived (center). In the distance are the homes of the Spanish.

While the relationship between the Spanish government and the Apalachee chiefs worked well, the relationship between the Spanish colonists and the Apalachee was at times strained. One missionary working at San Luis wrote:

It became customary for many settlers to compel Indian men and women to work for them, often without pay. Juana Caterina de Florencia, the wife of deputy-governor Jacinto Roque Pérez, was one of the worst offenders in this regard, requiring the village of San Luis to furnish six women for the grinding of meal every day without payment, another Indian to bring in a daily pitcher of milk from the country, and other services.

A priest living in Saint Augustine noted:

Each year from Apalachee alone more than three hundred are brought to the fort [in Saint Augustine] at the time of the planting of the corn, carrying their food and the merchandise of the soldiers on their shoulders . . . some on arrival die and those who survive [often] do not return to their homes because the governor and the other officials detain them in the fort so they may serve them and this without paying them a wage.

From San Luis, mission work continued to expand west into the land controlled by the Apalachicola Indians on the banks of what is today the Apalachicola River and extending into present-day Alabama. By the late 1600s, there were more than 20,000 Indians living in the mission system. In 1675 Gabriel Diaz Vara Calderón, Bishop of Cuba, visited most of the missions in Florida. He wrote:

bishop—an official of the Catholic church that oversees priests

*There are 13,152 Christianized Indians to whom I adminis-
tered the holy sacrament of confirmation. . . . They sleep on the
ground, and in their houses only on a frame made of reed bars,
which they call barbacoa, with a bear skin laid upon it and
without any cover, the fire they build in the center of the house
serving in place of a blanket. They call the house bujío. It is a
hut made in round form, of straw, without a window and with
a doorway. . . . Whatever they . . . [hunt or grow] they bring
to the principal cacique [chief], in order that he shall divide it.*

*These Indians do not covet riches, nor do they esteem silver or
gold, coins of which do not circulate among them, and their
only barter is the exchange of one commodity for another,
which exchange they call rescate. The most common articles of
trade are knives, scissors, axes, hoes, hatchets, large bronze rat-
tles, glass beads, blankets which they call congas, pieces of
rough cloth, garments and other trifles.*

The missions lasted into the 1700s, but their decline
began much earlier. Disease killed thousands of Indians.
Wars in Europe weakened the Spanish government.
Florida began to receive fewer supplies and less attention
and financial and military support from Spain. At the same
time, the English and the French were gaining power
exploring and colonizing the New World.

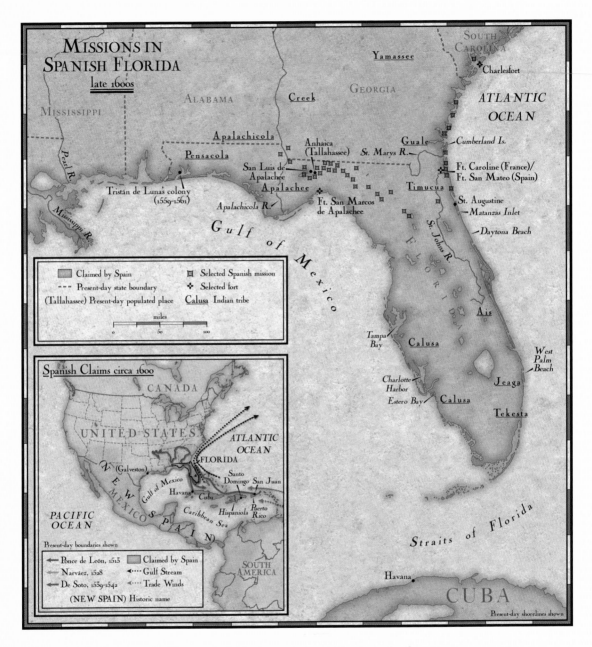

MISSIONS IN SPANISH FLORIDA
late 1600s

MISSISSIPPI

ALABAMA

Creek

GEORGIA

Yamassee

SOUTH CAROLINA

Charlesfort

ATLANTIC OCEAN

Apalachicola

Pensacola

Anhaica (Tallahassee)

St. Marys R.

Guale

Cumberland Is.

San Luis de Apalachee

Apalachee

Timucua

Ft. Caroline (France)/ Ft. San Mateo (Spain)

Tristán de Luna's colony (1559-1561)

Apalachicola R.

Ft. San Marcos de Apalachee

St. Augustine

Matanzas Inlet

Daytona Beach

Pearl R.

Mississippi R.

Gulf of Mexico

FLORIDA

St. Johns R.

Ais

Tampa Bay

Calusa

West Palm Beach

Charlotte Harbor

Estero Bay

Calusa

Jeaga

Tekesta

Legend:
- ▨ Claimed by Spain
- - - Present-day state boundary
- (Tallahassee) Present-day populated place
- ▨ Selected Spanish mission
- ✦ Selected fort
- Calusa Indian tribe

miles
0   50   100

Spanish Claims circa 1600

CANADA

UNITED STATES

ATLANTIC OCEAN

FLORIDA

(Galveston)

NEW MEXICO

PACIFIC OCEAN

(SPAIN)

Gulf of Mexico

Havana

Cuba

Santo Domingo

San Juan

Hispaniola

Puerto Rico

Caribbean Sea

SOUTH AMERICA

Present-day boundaries shown

- ← Ponce de León, 1513
- ← Narváez, 1528
- ← De Soto, 1539-1542
- ▨ Claimed by Spain
- ···· Gulf Stream
- ···· Trade Winds

(NEW SPAIN) Historic name

Straits of Florida

Havana

CUBA

Present-day shorelines shown

With the voyage of Ponce de León in 1513, Spain became the first European power to claim land in what is now the United States. Florida's strategic location along the Gulf Stream and at the entrance to the Caribbean helped protect Spanish treasure ships. Early settlement centered on a string of missions extending out from St. Augustine northward along the Atlantic coast into Georgia and westward across northern Florida to the region surrounding modern Tallahassee.

CHAPTER FOUR

Pressure from the French and English

1670 — 1713

FLORIDA COMES UNDER PRESSURE *from the French and English as Spain struggles to defend its empire abroad.*

s early as 1586, the English had attempted to build colonies in North America. Aware of Spain's position in Florida, the English settled far to the north in what is today Virginia and North Carolina. As English colonies prospered and expanded

OPPOSITE: A Spanish monk erects a cross on the site of a new mission with the help of Apalachee Indians.

along the northern and central Atlantic coast, England pushed south toward Florida to claim more land. In 1660, King Charles II of England approved a new English colony called Carolina. The colony contained the coastal land that would become present-day North Carolina, South Carolina, and Georgia and extended west to the Pacific Ocean.

Spain believed that its claim to Florida included the land of this new Carolina colony and that the English were invading. The Spanish tried to resolve the dispute through diplomacy, but the English continued to move closer and closer. Spanish Florida's defenses were low. Spain, still at war with England in Europe and the Caribbean, did not send enough men to replace those who had died or deserted, nor did it send enough money or supplies. There was little the Spanish in Florida could do to prevent the English advance.

diplomacy—the act of resolving disagreements through discussion, rather than war or other forms of hostility

In 1668 Robert Searles, an English privateer, attacked and burned Saint Augustine. By the time of Searles's attack, only 130 Spanish troops remained in Florida. Searles's attack killed at least 60 of the Spanish soldiers and some women and children.

After Searles's attack, Spain finally decided to build a stone fortress at Saint Augustine. But two years later, in 1670, construction still had not begun. Then news reached Florida that the English were constructing a fort and town at Charleston, in present-day South Carolina. Charleston was less than two days' sail from Saint Augustine. Fear of English attack from Charleston motivated the Spanish to begin building the fort and to send more soldiers to protect the city.

Construction of the stone fort at Saint Augustine, named Castillo de San Marcos, began in 1672. Stoneworkers from Cuba and hundreds of Indians from the missions were sent to build it. Spain sent 100 new soldiers to man the fort and guard it during construction. Spain also sent a fleet of ships from Cuba to attack Charleston. The attack was not successful, but it did force the British to reinforce their position before pushing again toward Florida.

Saint Augustine, the capital of the colony, was now well protected. Castillo de San Marcos was soon surrounded by rows of small houses, most built from coquina along narrow dirt roads.

COQUINA

CASTILLO DE SAN MARCOS WAS built from coquina, a type of rock found near Saint Augustine. Coquina is formed from sand and the shells of tiny sea creatures. As the creatures die, their shells pile up. Over time, water, sand, and more shells push down on the shells, compacting them into a rock similar to limestone. Workers quarried the coquina on nearby Anastasia Island and ferried the stone back to Saint Augustine.

The Spanish had never worked with stone of this type and had no idea how strong it would be. In 1702, when the fort was finally tested by enemy fire, the cannonballs that struck the fort sank into the walls but did not destroy them. A frustrated English soldier wrote that the walls *"give way to the cannon ball as though you would stick a knife in cheese."*

The stone houses were sturdy in the winter and in hurricane season, yet still cool in the summer. Most of the houses had small, walled-in yards attached.

To protect the western missions, they constructed a large wooden fort on Florida's Gulf Coast, near present-day Tallahassee. The fort, named Fort San Marcos de Apalachee, was constructed several miles south of the mission at San Luis. The fort protected not only the western missions, but also the harbor, allowing ships to safely carry food grown at Mission San Luis de Apalachee to Saint Augustine and then on to Cuba.

THE FRENCH APPROACH FROM THE WEST

Spain did little else to colonize the Gulf Coast of Florida. In 1682, René-Robert Cavelier, Sieur de La Salle, a French explorer, fur trapper, and trader, reached the mouth of the Mississippi River along the Gulf of Mexico. When news of his expedition reached France, he was asked to establish a colony at the mouth of the river. Accounts of his voyage also reached Spain. Leaders of both countries knew that whoever settled the mouth of the Mississippi River could control trade in the area. They also knew that a French settlement there would separate Spanish Florida from other Spanish territories, including New Spain and present-day Texas.

A hand-colored woodcut shows French explorer René-Robert Cavelier, Sieur de La Salle, and members of his crew traveling down the Mississippi River. La Salle's discovery of the mouth of the river in 1682 prompted French interest in the area and made the Spanish anxious about their control of the region.

La Salle returned in 1684 with four ships and 300 colonists. But he was unable to find the mouth of the Mississippi River, and continued along the Gulf Coast, ending up about 400 miles (640 km) west of the Mississippi. A few weeks later, a storm caused La Salle's ship to run aground in present-day Matagorda Bay, near Corpus Christi, Texas. There, La Salle founded Fort St. Louis for the French, and ordered several houses built. Soon after, La Salle made several unsuccessful attempts to find the mouth of the Mississippi. La Salle's failures caused his men to doubt his leadership, and in 1687, he was killed in a mutiny. Without reinforcements, the colony

mutiny—revolt against a lawful authority

failed. Eventually the news reached Spain and France. Both countries were now in a race to find the mouth of the Mississippi and occupy the region surrounding it.

Over the next five years, the French sent at least seven expeditions to the area. The Spanish sent eleven. Both countries explored by land and sea. But the mouth of the river was not found until a Spanish expedition in late 1689. At nearly the same time, another Spanish expedition located the remains of Tristán de Luna's failed colony near present-day Pensacola. Juan Jordán de Reina, an officer on one expedition to the area, described Pensacola Bay in his diary as *"the best bay I have ever seen in my life."*

Native Americans camp along the shore of White Sand Bluffs on Isle de St. Rose (Santa Rosa Island) near Pensacola, first seen by the Spanish around 1540. Fish are drying on a rack behind the "lean-to," and woven baskets for gathering food can be seen on the left.

Descriptions of Pensacola Bay reached King Charles II in Spain. The Spanish government did not want to build a fort at the mouth of both the Mississippi River and Pensacola Bay. While each area had its own advantages, Pensacola appeared easier to defend and was a better harbor. In 1698, Andrés de Arriola, an experienced Spanish military leader, and de Reina were sent to Pensacola Bay to establish a colony. De Reina sailed from Cuba with a small force and arrived on November 17, 1698. Arriola sailed from Mexico and arrived four days later with nearly 400 men.

Arriola expected the French to send a large force to attack his position at Pensacola. He knew he needed to build a fort to defend the colony, but he was afraid that the French would arrive before the fort was completed. So Arriola decided to outwit the enemy. Rather than build the entire fort, Arriola had his men work only on the wall of the fort that was visible from the water. In January 1699, the French arrived at Pensacola, but Arriola refused to let them anchor in Pensacola Bay. He allowed several French soldiers to come ashore to get water and supplies, but he did not allow them near the fort. Tricked into believing that the Spanish had constructed a large fort, the French returned to their ships and sailed west. Captain Jamie Frank, a military engineer who was in charge of building the Spanish fort, wrote in his journal: *"I built the front facing the camp to look so good that the one who sees it could infer*

military engineer—a designer of forts, harbors, and other fortified positions

*that an attack on it will be a bloody business. And, that is how the . . .
French squadron saw it."*

The French went on to build a fort on the Gulf Coast
of present-day Mississippi. In the years that followed, the
French also established colonies at what are now Mobile,
Alabama, and Biloxi, Mississippi, west of Pensacola.

MOORE ATTACKS SAINT AUGUSTINE

In 1701 King Charles II of Spain died. The next year, war
broke out in Europe over who would take over the Spanish
throne. Charles had left the throne to Philip V, grandson of
Louis XIV of France. The English feared that this would
cause France and Spain one day to be combined into a large
and very powerful empire. To prevent this possibility,
England attacked both the French and Spanish in what
became known as the War of the Spanish Succession in
Europe and Queen Anne's War in North America, where
the English fought the French in the north and the Spanish
in the south.

Shortly after war was declared, the English in Carolina
prepared to attack Saint Augustine. Colonel James Moore,
governor of Carolina, commanded a force of more than 500
soldiers as well as Indian allies. Though an official count
was never taken, letters from both the Spanish and English
say that Moore's force may have exceeded 1,200 men.

As Moore's troops made their way south from Charleston, they attacked Spanish missions and outposts. News of the size and power of the force reached the newly appointed Spanish governor, Don Joseph de Zúñiga y Zerda. Zúñiga sent messengers to Cuba to ask for aid in fighting the coming attack. He ordered more than 1,500 people, including all the civilians and many of the local Indians, to take shelter in Castillo de San Marcos. Once inside, Zúñiga ordered the moat surrounding the fortress to be drained. Local farmers were instructed to bring their cattle to the moat so the citizens would have a large supply of food if they had to stay in the fortress for a long time.

moat—a trench around a fort or castle that can be filled with water

On November 10, 1702, Moore and his forces reached Saint Augustine. They took control of the empty city and began bombarding the fortress. The coquina walls did not crumble. He decided to lay siege to the fortress, blocking all supplies from reaching it by land. Moore hoped that after several weeks the food, water, and other supplies in the fortress would run out. Then Zúñiga would have no choice but to surrender.

siege—a military tactic designed to force surrender by blockading a town and preventing supplies from reaching it

On December 29, 1702, nearly 50 days after the siege began, four ships arrived from Havana, Cuba, to reinforce Zúñiga. Moore realized that the ships from Cuba carried not only soldiers but also supplies, which would allow Zúñiga to last probably another 50 days. Moore decided to withdraw from the city. As his troops left, they burned the city to the ground. The only buildings that were not totally destroyed were Castillo de San Marcos, a church, and a few smaller buildings.

On the way back to Charleston, Moore burned every mission or outpost he passed as well as several Indian villages. The missions were never rebuilt. The Spanish focused instead on rebuilding Saint Augustine. They also extended thick walls from Castillo de San Marcos to surround the entire city and protect it from future attacks.

In 1703, Moore, still angry about his loss at Saint Augustine, began another series of attacks, this time into central and western Florida. Moore raised an army of 80 English soldiers and more than 1,500 Creek Indians. This time he avoided major outposts, including the fort at San Marcos and the mission at San Luis de Apalachee. Instead, he attacked smaller missions and villages. After more than a year of constant attacks on the Apalachee missions, Moore returned to Carolina in late 1704 with more than 4,000 slaves, mostly women and children. He reported that he had killed hundreds of Indian men and more than 1,000 women and children. He had also killed any Spanish missionaries and soldiers he encountered.

By 1706, the Spanish abandoned Fort San Marcos and the mission at San Luis, withdrawing their troops and the remaining mission Indians to Saint Augustine and its

census—a count of the population of an area

surrounding areas. In 1713, a census of the remaining Christian Indians in Spanish Florida counted only 400, who all lived in an Indian village called Nombre de Dios north of Saint Augustine. Of the more than 20,000 Indians living in the mission system less than ten years earlier, more than 8,000 had been taken as slaves by the Carolinians, thousands had been killed, and others had fled the missions, joining the tribes to the northwest. By the end of 1713, the mission system was completely destroyed. Pensacola was a small outpost. Spain's true power in Florida did not extend beyond the range of the Castillo de San Marcos's guns.

CHAPTER FIVE

Imperial Outpost

1713 — 1763

SPAIN IS FORCED TO DEFEND FLORIDA *once again from British advancement, this time from the Georgia colony. Britain's victory in the French and Indian War forces the Spanish to turn over control of Florida to the British.*

 y the time the wars in Europe were over, there were fewer than 1,000 people living in all of Spanish Florida. The Spanish in Florida were no longer a threat to the British colonies. But over time, as the British advanced, Indian groups were driven south into Florida. This growing Indian population greatly

OPPOSITE: Chiefs of Indian tribes who banded together to fight the British in the Yamassee War in 1715 lead their troops into battle.

concerned the British colonies. While the British had a working relationship with the Creek, the Spanish and French had better relationships with most other Indian tribes in southeastern North America.

Many of the Apalachee Indians who had fled Moore and the Creek attacks settled between Carolina and Florida. They were joined by the Yamassee, a rival tribe of the Creek in the lands between present-day north Florida and South Carolina. If the French or Spanish raised an army of Indians as Moore had done, they could easily attack Charleston and other cities in the British colonies. To prevent this possibility, the British made trading with Indians a priority.

Over time, the British increased their prices for goods traded to the Indians. When Indians could not pay for these items, many tribes found themselves in debt. Some British traders began taking Yamassee and Apalachee women and children as slaves in payment for the debts. This practice soon resulted in conflict that would escalate into war.

THE YAMASSEE WAR

In spring 1715, the Yamassee, Apalachee, and several smaller tribes banded together. They attacked British settlements throughout Carolina, killing hundreds of colonists and burning their homes in what became known as the Yamassee War. The British were greatly outnumbered. The Indians drove the settlers back toward the Atlantic coast and northern Carolina and Virginia.

The Yamassee tried to convince other Indian tribes to join them. The British had the support of the Creek, but feared that a large, powerful tribe called the Cherokee would join the Yamassee. The British offered to give the Cherokee guns, ammunition, and other goods in exchange for their support. The combined British and Cherokee force drove the Yamassee and Apalachee south into northern Florida. Not only had the British attempt to form good relationships with the Yamassee failed, but it also strengthened Spanish Florida by adding hundreds of Indians to its shrinking population.

THE GEORGIA COLONY

The land between Spanish Florida and Britain's Carolina colony was claimed by both the Spanish and British. Since the fall of the Spanish missions in the area, neither country had done much to secure its claim to the area, which became known as the "debatable land."

In 1732 James Edward Oglethorpe, a proven military leader and former member of Britain's Parliament, drafted a charter asking for permission to establish a British colony in North America. This new colony, named Georgia, was located just north of Florida in the debatable land. Oglethorpe planned it as a buffer between the Spanish region and the British colonies that would help protect the town of Charleston.

Parliament—a part of government that makes laws

In February 1733, Oglethorpe and 114 settlers arrived along the coast of Georgia at Yamacraw Bluffs. They quickly set to work building a walled city named Savannah. Oglethorpe feared a direct attack by the Spanish. His fears were confirmed in 1735 when the Spanish briefly attacked Savannah then retreated to Saint Augustine. In response, Oglethorpe built a series of outposts and began scouting the northern border of Florida. Satisfied with the security of his position, Oglethorpe pushed toward Florida. Within a year he began constructing forts within the borders of Spanish Florida.

AFRICANS
in Spanish Florida

SLAVERY WAS LONG PRACTICED ACROSS THE SPANISH Empire. There was large-scale importation of black slaves, but not all black Spaniards were slaves. Some black slaves were granted their freedom after years of service or the death of their master. Others were the offspring of interracial unions and were granted freedom by their white fathers. Over time, the black population grew and became an accepted part of Spanish society. In fact, two black men, Juan Gárrido and Juan González, were members of de León's 1513 expedition. Blacks also sailed with de Soto.

In 1683, Florida's governor created a militia company of 48 free blacks in Saint Augustine. The total free black population of the city was nearly 200.

Villa Gracia Real de Santa Teresa de Mose

King Philip V of Spain was angered when the new British colony of Savannah was founded on lands he believed belonged to him. In 1733, he announced that slaves who escaped their masters in the British colonies, entered Florida, and accepted the Catholic faith would be freed. This offer attracted escaped slaves from across the British colonies to Florida and greatly angered slave owners to the north.

Fort Mose was home to the first free black settlement in North America. Officials in Spanish Florida in the 1680s recruited former black slaves like this man to fill the ranks of an all-black militia.

Many former slaves moved to Saint Augustine or the area around it. The free blacks quickly became accepted members of Saint Augustine society. In 1738, Don Manuel de Montiano, governor of Florida, offered a large group of former slaves a plot of land about 2 miles (3.2 km) north of Saint Augustine. One requirement of taking the land was that they build a town and fort there. The Spanish gave the free blacks weapons and supplies to build the wooden fort. The new town, known as Gracia Real de Santa Teresa de Mose, or Fort Mose, was overseen by a black military captain named Francisco Menéndez. He had earlier led the black militia company in Saint Augustine. Fort Mose grew to a population of nearly 200. In addition to being a productive farming town, it served as a key defense point for the city of Saint Augustine.

THE WAR OF JENKINS'S EAR

In the early 1730s, Spain allowed British ships to pass through the Spanish-controlled Caribbean, but they were not allowed to trade in Spanish ports. Spanish ships frequently stopped British ships and examined their cargo to make sure they followed this rule. In 1731, Captain Juan de Leon Fandino of Spain stopped the *Rebecca*, a merchant ship under the command of Robert Jenkins, off the coast of Havana. Fandino and his men boarded the *Rebecca*. Jenkins and Fandino got into an argument. Fandino ordered Jenkins tied up while his ship was searched. When Jenkins resisted, Fandino cut off his ear. Fandino's men found illegal cargo and destroyed it, and Jenkins was allowed to return to England.

An English engraving shows the incident that touched off the War of Jenkins's Ear. Spanish soldiers from the *San Antonio* (left) boarded Captain Jenkins's vessel and engaged in an argument that resulted in the Spanish captain cutting off Jenkins's ear.

In August 1738, seven years after the event, Jenkins was asked to tell his story to Parliament. Jenkins brought his severed ear, which he had preserved, in a bottle. His tale angered many members of Parliament who shortly after voted to declare war on Spain. This war became known as the War of Jenkins's Ear. With war declared, however, it was only a question of time before the Spanish or British launched an attack in Georgia or Florida. The British struck first.

In 1739, Oglethorpe assembled a force of more than 1,400 men, including British soldiers, volunteers from Georgia and the Carolinas, and Creek and Cherokee Indians, to invade Florida and attack Saint Augustine. Oglethorpe, who had studied Moore's defeat, arranged for a blockade by the British Navy that would prevent supplies and reinforcements from reaching Saint Augustine by sea.

blockade—a movement of ships or troops used to prevent reinforcements or supplies from reaching a location

Smaller parties ahead of Oglethorpe's main force attacked Spanish outposts along the Georgia border. Spanish soldiers stationed there retreated to Saint Augustine. By the time Oglethorpe's force reached Fort Mose, it was abandoned, and all weapons had been removed. Still, Oglethorpe left a group of about 140 men there.

Spanish reinforcements, which included 150 troops and supplies, arrived in Saint Augustine several days before Oglethorpe's main force. Upon his arrival, Oglethorpe ordered his cannon set on Anastasia Island, across the bay from Saint Augustine. Most of his troops camped on the mainland, back from the city walls.

The British cannon bombarded Castillo de San Marcos for 38 days. Amazingly, the walls held. British cannonballs hit the thick coquina walls of the fort and rolled to the ground outside. At night the Spanish collected the cannonballs. Those that were still in working order were fired back at the British. Oglethorpe hoped that the Spanish would run out of supplies and be forced to surrender before more reinforcements arrived.

In early June, supplies began to run low in the fortress. Governor Montiano estimated that the Spanish only had enough food for several weeks. On the night of June 26, 1740, Montiano sent a force of former slaves, Indians, and Spanish soldiers to retake Fort Mose. Under cover of night they stormed the fort and killed or captured more than 100 British soldiers. News of the attack on Fort Mose reached Oglethorpe. Oglethorpe pulled back and retreated to Georgia.

The Spanish then began planning an attack on Georgia. In June 1742, Montiano left Saint Augustine and sailed north with a force of 52 ships and more than 2,000 men drawn from across New Spain.

Oglethorpe had less than 700 men in Georgia—he was outnumbered nearly three to one. He did not have a fortress like Castillo de San Marcos for defense, and he believed that he would surely be defeated in open combat. His only option was to ambush the Spanish force. Oglethorpe realized that the Spanish intended first to attack his forces at Fort Frederica, a military base located 60 miles (96 km) south of Savannah. The path to Fort Frederica was a narrow raised trail that cut through a wide marsh. He planned to use this location for his ambush.

On July 7, 1742, the Spanish sent a group of 200 soldiers down the road toward Fort Frederica. Oglethorpe had 60 men in hiding in the marsh on the side of the road. Once the Spanish group was surrounded, Oglethorpe's men opened fire. Captain Don Antonio Barba was killed almost immediately. The battle, later known as the Battle of Bloody Marsh, lasted less than an hour. Spanish survivors retreated to the main force and described the ambush. Governor Montiano decided to fall back to Saint Augustine.

James Oglethorpe's forces battle the Spanish along the swampy path to Fort Frederica, south of Savannah, in a skirmish known as the Battle of Bloody Marsh.

Over the next 15 years, the British and the Spanish continued to reinforce their positions. Occasionally they made small raids on each other's territory, but no other major attacks were attempted.

Spain Loses Florida

In 1756, Britain and its Indian allies declared war on the French and their native allies. In Europe the war was known as the Seven Years' War, but in North America it became known as the French and Indian War. Most of the war was fought far to the north of Florida. But in 1762, Spain entered the war on the side of France. The British quickly used this as an excuse to attack and occupy the Spanish port at Havana, Cuba. The Spanish were little help to the French, and by 1763, the war was over. The British were victorious.

Florida was important to the Spanish, but not as important as Havana. Havana was one of the oldest and largest cities in the Americas. It was also where the Spanish treasure fleets carrying silver and gold met before forming convoys to return to Spain. Florida, with the exception of Saint Augustine, was mostly undeveloped wilderness. As part of the Treaty of Paris of 1763, which ended the war, the Spanish traded control of Florida to the British in exchange for the return of Havana. After 198 years of Spanish rule, Florida became a British possession.

CHAPTER SIX

Florida in the British Empire

1763 — 1775

FLORIDA BECOMES TWO COLONIES *under the British, East Florida and West Florida. The colonies remain underpopulated until the mid 1700s when indigo plantations become profitable, and the town of Saint Augustine grows and prospers.*

he region of Florida that the Spanish signed over to the British was much larger than the state of Florida today. It included all of present-day Florida and extended along the Gulf of Mexico all the way to the Mississippi River, including parts of

OPPOSITE: After the 1763 Treaty of Paris gave Britain control of Florida, Pensacola was made the capital of West Florida and became a thriving port city.

present-day Alabama, Mississippi, and Louisiana. The British divided the region into two colonies: East Florida and West Florida. East Florida extended from the St. Marys River around the entire Florida peninsula to the Apalachicola River. West Florida was a strip of land bordering the Gulf Coast from the Apalachicola River to the Mississippi River. Saint Augustine was named the capital of East Florida. James Grant was appointed its governor. Pensacola was selected as the capital of West Florida and was governed by George Johnstone.

When Britain gained control of Florida from Spain in 1763, it divided the region into two colonies: East and West Florida. At the same time, to prevent future conflicts between Native Americans and colonists, the British established a boundary called the Royal Proclamation Line separating Indian territory and lands that could be settled by colonists. According to the Proclamation, the Floridas were in the region open for settlement.

In September 1763, Lieutenant Colonel James Robertson, a British soldier, toured Saint Augustine as part of a formal inspection of East and West Florida. He described the city as *"a struggling little settlement, unproductive of any supplies save fish, and with the ground overgrown with weeds."*

As part of the agreement between Spain and Britain, the Spanish citizens, former slaves, and Catholic Indians were allowed to freely leave the new colonies before the British took control. Most moved to Cuba. Of the 3,000 residents of Saint Augustine, only four stayed. Before they left, the Spanish even exhumed the bodies of their dead governors for reburial in Cuba. Pensacola was also handed over to the British almost entirely vacant. Governors Johnstone and Grant realized that if they wanted their colonies to become successful, they would need colonists to move there.

land grant—a deed giving ownership of a piece of land, usually after certain obligations have been fulfilled, such as farming the land, living on it, or settling additional people on it

To attract colonists, the British began giving land grants to people who were willing to live and farm on a plot of land. Colonists only had to pay a small fee to have the land surveyed and their grant recorded. Over 2 million acres (810,000 ha) of land in East Florida were claimed by British citizens living in London, but few of the new owners moved onto the land. Land in West Florida was populated by people who came from other British colonies. They moved onto the land to farm it.

THE EAST FLORIDA SOCIETY

Back in London, many people who registered large land grants were not sure exactly what to do with their new plots of land. Many of the grant holders formed a club called the East Florida Society. The society met monthly to discuss ideas for recruiting colonists and planning the colony.

Members of the society formed into two groups with different opinions about the best way to develop East Florida. The first group became known as Musquito University. Led by a rich banker and merchant named Richard Oswald, the members believed that East Florida should be used to grow sugar. They favored importing slaves from Africa to work large sugar plantations. The second group became known as Grant College because it followed Governor Grant's vision for East Florida. Grant thought that Florida plantations were better suited to growing indigo, a plant that was used to make a blue dye. People across the British Empire were willing to pay a lot of money for cloth and clothing dyed with indigo. Indigo could be grown profitably on small plantations without a large number of slaves.

A 1799 engraving of an indigo plant, a crop that brought prosperity to British Florida

ROLLESTOWN AND NEW SMYRNA

Land grant holders needed to persuade many different groups of people to move to Florida to work their land. For example, they tried to convince French and German Protestants and British citizens living in other colonies. They also tried to attract people too poor to pay for their own passage to the Colonies to settle in Florida as indentured servants. Indentured servants agreed to work for a person for a set amount of time in exchange for food, shelter, and paid passage to America.

In 1764, Denys Rolle, a wealthy landowner, received a land grant for 20,000 acres (8,100 ha) on the St. Johns River. He published a pamphlet describing his plan for his Florida plantation and distributed it to many poor laborers in London. He promised to provide education for their children and to encourage Christianity. He described his land grant as *"the most precious jewel of his majesty's American dominions."*

In the fall of 1764, Rolle established a small town 30 miles (48 km) southwest of Saint Augustine. It became known as Rollestown. Rolle and his settlers fought from the start. They claimed that he had lied to them and made promises in his pamphlet that he did not keep. Most of his settlers deserted him and ended up moving to Saint Augustine. By 1773, Rollestown was abandoned, and Rolle returned to England.

In 1766, Andrew Turnbull, a British doctor who had been living in Greece and Turkey for several years, approached the East Florida Society with an idea for a large East Florida settlement. He proposed sailing to Greece to recruit settlers. At that time, many people in Greece were living in harsh conditions. Food was in short supply, and many people disagreed with the policies of the Greek government. Turnbull thought that the climate in Florida was similar enough to Greece's climate to allow settlers to grow grapes for wine and olives as they had in Greece. Turnbull promised that with a little support he could deliver settlers.

Turnbull was much more successful than he thought he would be. He was able to recruit 300 Greek settlers to go to Florida with him. Turnbull also brought about 200 settlers from southern Italy to Florida. The majority of his recruits, however, came from Spain's Mediterranean island of Minorca, where many were suffering from starvation due to a famine.

While Turnbull was recruiting in Greece, some of his partners had gone ahead to Florida to make preparations for the new settlement, called New Smyrna. Unfortunately, his partners did not expect 1,500 settlers to arrive. When the newcomers landed, there was nowhere near enough food, shelter, or supplies for them all. The settlers considered their situation and rebelled. A group of them broke open the ware-house to feed themselves, and another group stole a ship and planned to escape to Cuba. Turnbull called in the British soldiers from Saint Augustine to regain control. Two of the ring-leaders of the rebellion were hanged. The rest of the settlers went back to work. Within a year, half of them were dead from disease and lack of food. The rest struggled to survive until their indenture agreements ran out.

Dr. Andrew Turnbull, founder of Florida's New Smyrna settlement

In 1771 a census was taken in East Florida. It officially recorded 288 white men living in the colony. The settlers at New Smyrna were not officially counted, nor were Indians or slaves, but estimates based on letters and slave shipments suggest that there were fewer than 3,000 non-native people living in East Florida. The population of East Florida after ten years was still about the same as it was under Spanish rule.

West Florida attracted more colonists. By 1771 there were more than 3,700 white settlers and nearly 1,200 black slaves there. But even this population was far too small to build a strong colony, especially in the face of an Indian population that greatly outnumbered the settlers.

THE SEMINOLE

As British colonies in the Carolinas and Georgia expanded, even the Creek who had long been British allies began to be pushed out. Some moved west, but others headed south into Florida and began to join together with other tribes, including the Yamassee and Apalachee. By 1750, a large group of these Indians had gathered south of present-day Gainesville at a town they called Cuscowilla. The Indians sheltered escaped slaves and often took part in cattle and horse raids against both the British and Spanish. These Indians became known as the Seminole, which comes from the Creek word *Ishti Seminole*, meaning outlaw. The Creek Indians called this group Seminole because they refused to acknowledge Creek authority.

Even though the British had a long history of trading with Creek tribes that many of the Seminole had once belonged to, the British feared a Seminole attack. They also feared that the Seminole would become allies of Spain. To prevent this, the British increased their trading. The Seminole, however, also traded with the Spanish. The tribe acted like a buffer between the two empires.

FLORIDA PROSPERS

As indigo plantations began to become profitable, Saint Augustine grew. The British moved into old Spanish homes, keeping the original architectural style but adding fireplaces and chimneys. Ships regularly carried cargo of indigo to New York and loads of lumber, harvested from local woodlands, to South Carolina. British colonies in the Caribbean began shipping tropical goods such as sugar to Saint Augustine. From there it was shipped to northern colonies. Saint Augustine began building ties to northern colonies and appeared ready to become a major shipping location for the British colonies.

The people of Saint Augustine rejoiced in their new prosperity. Governor Grant himself once wrote, *"There is not so gay a town in America as this at the present, music and dancing mad."* But as the 1770s continued, changes in Britain's 13 Colonies would soon alter life in Florida. ✱

CHAPTER SEVEN

Florida and the Revolution

1775 — 1784

FLORIDA BECOMES A DESTINATION *for Loyalists during the Revolutionary War. The 1783 Treaty of Paris, ending the American Revolution, returns Florida to the Spanish.*

The two Florida colonies had much smaller populations than Britain's other colonies in North America. The residents, who were separated by large distances, did not elect public officials. The governor of each of the Florida colonies selected council members to help him rule. When Great Britain increased

OPPOSITE: British soldiers fighting the Spanish in the Battle of Pensacola during the Revolutionary War meet with defeat. Dead and wounded soldiers can be seen in the foreground, and Spanish ships dot the bay.

taxes on certain common goods, such as tea and paper, people in the northern colonies organized and complained to their elected officials. The people of Florida, however, small in number and dependent upon Britain for protection, continued to pay the taxes. In 1765, Florida did not send representatives to the Stamp Act Congress, a meeting of delegates from other colonies who believed that the British taxes were unfair. Nor did either Florida colony send representatives to the Continental Congress in Philadelphia, where 13 other colonies decided in 1776 to declare their independence from England.

By signing the Declaration of Independence, the 13 American colonies declared themselves independent states, free from British laws and taxes. This move worried many residents of Florida. They had hoped that trade with the other colonies would help them prosper, and they feared that the independent states would refuse to trade with them. When news of the Declaration of Independence reached Saint Augustine, many residents rallied in the streets in support of the British government. They dressed up dummies to look like colonial leaders Samuel Adams and John Hancock and burned them in the street.

Once the Revolutionary War began, residents of the 13 states worried about what would happen in Florida. Patriot leaders in Georgia and South Carolina feared that the British would again use their relationship with the Creek in Florida to raise an Indian army to attack the southern states. Many

Loyalist—a colonist who remained loyal to Britain during the Revolution; also known as a Tory

Loyalists fled the 13 rebellious states and moved to British Florida.

In 1777, American forces in Georgia began plans to capture the city of Saint Augustine and take control of Florida. An American commander, Colonel William Moultrie, assembled more than 2,000 troops and prepared to march on Florida. Luckily for the British and for the new governor of East Florida, Patrick Tonyn, who replaced retiring Governor Grant, British reinforcements arrived in Saint Augustine. Moultrie's forces, however, never made it to Saint Augustine. His small army contained many untrained volunteers. Communication was difficult, and sickness spread throughout the ranks. His army fell apart before it reached the East Florida border, and he had no choice but to return to Savannah.

In 1778, the Americans prepared an even larger force in Savannah under the command of General Robert Howe. In late June, the American force headed south in waves. The first group was made up of 500 volunteers, followed closely by another 900 volunteers. The main force remained a full day's march behind. Unknown to the Americans, most of

General Robert Howe of the Continental Army

the British force in Saint Augustine, nearly 500 trained soldiers under the command of General James Marc Prevost, was marching north. Scouts warned Prevost of the approaching American troops. He waited for them at a bridge that crossed a small stream called Alligator Creek.

The Americans attacked but could not push the British from the bridge. The volunteer force fell back, warned the advancing American troops about the British force, and retreated to Savannah. The British retreated to Saint Augustine and remained there until January 1779, when General Prevost successfully attacked Georgia and occupied the city of Savannah.

With Savannah under British control, the Florida residents' fear of an invasion by the Continental Army was calmed. East Florida served as a major supply base for the British Army throughout the remainder of the American Revolution.

SPAIN ATTACKS WEST FLORIDA

West Florida was quiet during the first few years of the American Revolution. In 1779, however, Spain entered the war as an ally of the United States. General Bernardo de Gálvez, the governor of Louisiana, marched east from New Orleans with an army of more than 7,000 soldiers. Gálvez's army included French, Spanish, Indians, and blacks from

Louisiana, Cuba, and Mexico. Within a month, he had captured six British forts and taken nearly 600 British prisoners. He did not count enemy deaths, but his army suffered only one casualty. The British began to worry.

In March 1780, Gálvez reached the British town and fort at Mobile. The city surrendered after four days of constant attack. The threat of British counterattack caused Gálvez to leave nearly half his force behind to defend Mobile and other forts he had taken along the way. On March 9, 1781, Gálvez and his force of nearly 5,000 men and 64 ships reached the city of Pensacola. The city was protected by British general Thomas Campbell, who commanded a force of more than 2,000 British soldiers and 1,000 Indian allies. They fought outside the city. It was not until May 1 that Gálvez was able to get his cannon into position to begin bombarding the fort. The battle lasted for eight days.

During the Revolutionary War, Creek leader Hopothle-Mico allied his tribe with the British in an unsuccessful attempt to defeat the Spanish at Pensacola.

Each night Gálvez moved his cannon, hoping for the shot that would break a wall or cause enough damage to allow his men to storm the fort. He never expected what finally happened. On the morning of May 8, a Spanish battery took aim at the fort, fired its cannon, and watched in surprise as a large portion of the wall collapsed. The shot landed in the open doorway of the main powder magazine in the fort and ignited the main supply of gunpowder, blowing a large hole in one of the walls of the fort. The explosion caused about 100 casualties. Many of the Loyalists and Indians supporting the British fled, deserting Campbell, whose force was now greatly outnumbered. On May 10, the British surrendered the city of Pensacola and, with it, the last British force in West Florida. The Spanish occupied West Florida until the end of the Revolution.

As the war turned and the British began to lose ground, more Loyalists moved to Saint Augustine. The British evacuated Savannah and then Charleston and took with them thousands of Loyalists and their slaves. In less than eight years, the population

William Bartram's TRAVELS

IN 1765, WILLIAM BARTRAM traveled to Florida with his father, John, who had been named King's Botanist to the Floridas. Growing up with a botanist, William was naturally drawn to plant life. He tried his hand at farming but had little success. In 1773, he began a four-year trek that took him across Florida as well as eight other British colonies. Throughout his journey, he kept a detailed journal of the animals, plants, and people he encountered. He carefully illustrated many of the living things he saw. In 1791, he published his journal titled "The Travels of William Bartram," which became one of the most popular accounts of its time.

of East Florida rose from nearly 4,000 in 1775 to 17,000 by the end of 1782. Governor Tonyn agreed to allow the people of the colony to elect a council of representatives. They also founded Florida's first newspaper, the *East Florida Gazette*. Still, the Floridians remained loyal to England.

In April 1783, word reached Saint Augustine that a peace treaty had been signed. The American Revolution was over. The 13 rebellious colonies had become the United States of America. To their shock, the people of Florida learned that as part of the Treaty of Paris, which ended the war, Britain agreed to return Florida to Spain.

The British government agreed to pay Floridians for their lost property and offered them land in the Bahamas. Most of the settlers accepted the deal and abandoned the colony. On July 14, 1784, almost exactly 21 years after the British flag went up, it came down. Florida was once again part of the Spanish Empire.

CHAPTER EIGHT

Toward Statehood

SPANISH FLORIDA BECOMES *a disorganized region with undefined borders and constant uprisings by American forces and Native Americans. In 1821, Florida becomes part of the United States.*

On June 27, 1784, General Vicente Manuel de Zespedes y Velasco arrived as the newly appointed Spanish governor of Florida. Zespedes encouraged the British residents of Florida to stay, though few did. He also encouraged the Spanish settlers who had left Florida when the British took control to come home. Nearly 500 returned from Cuba. By 1790 there were 2,000 civilians living in Florida. About 1,000 lived

OPPOSITE: Castillo de San Marcos, the fort at Saint Augustine, flies the flag of the United States for the first time on February 22, 1821.

in Saint Augustine, 600 in Pensacola, and 400 throughout the rest of Florida.

Zespedes knew it was important for his colony to have a good trading relationship with the United States. He welcomed merchant ships and sailors from the new country. One merchant in 1789 wrote, *"Our vessels are received with the greatest cordiality by the Spaniards. Governor Zespedes, pays the greatest attention to every American who comes properly recommended. . . . Flour and all kinds of provisions from the United States, find a good market here."*

While Zespedes did what he could to attract settlers, merchants, and traders, Spain continued to weaken. After years of war across the globe, the Spanish Empire lacked the resources to keep a large military force in Florida. Zespedes and many other Floridians began to fear an attack by the United States.

SLAVERY ISSUES

In 1790, U.S. Secretary of State Thomas Jefferson wrote to Zespedes complaining that the Spanish in Florida were harboring fugitive slaves. It had long been a Spanish policy to allow escaped slaves to live in Florida as free people. But to prevent a major disagreement with the larger and more powerful United States, Zespedes agreed to change Florida's laws. Fugitive slaves would no longer be protected.

African slaves became a large part of the population when Spain began offering free land grants to settlers from the United States. By 1804, nearly 750 settlers registered for land grants in Florida, bringing more than 4,000 slaves with them. They began to establish plantations along the St. Johns River and on the islands off the northeast Florida coast.

ANNA MAJIGEEN JAI KINGSLEY

ZEPHANIAH KINGSLEY OWNED AND OPERATED ONE OF THE largest plantations in Florida. It was located northeast of present-day Jacksonville. His plantation grew more than 200 acres (81 ha) of cotton.

In 1806, Kingsley purchased a 13-year-old slave named Anta Majigeen Jai. She had been born in what is now the country of Senegal in Africa. Kingsley cared deeply for Anta, whom he called Anna. They had three sons together. Though he never officially married her, he gave her and her children their freedom, a house, and slaves of their own. He also had her change her name to Anna Majigeen Jai Kingsley.

In 1837, Zephaniah moved Anna and her sons to Haiti, where he established another plantation. By this time, Florida had become part of the United States. With the new government came new laws making interracial marriage illegal and racism part of the culture.

In 1843, Zephaniah died, and Anna took over the day-to-day operations of the plantation. Her plantation was very profitable. Four years later, she returned to Florida and purchased another plantation. When she died in 1870 at the age of 77, she was one of the richest landowners in Florida.

BILLY BOWLEGS

Florida remained under great pressure. The western borders were poorly defined, causing the United States and Spain to disagree over who controlled parts of the area. The region was populated by Indians and escaped slaves, while pirates, the British, and the Americans pushed in from the north and the southern coast.

Pirates off the coast of Florida divide the spoils from their attacks on ships passing through the Gulf of Mexico.

In 1800, William Augustus Bowles, known as Billy Bowlegs, rallied the support of a large number of Creek and Seminole Indians in western Florida. He was a former British soldier and Creek leader. Some saw Bowles as a pirate, others as a hero.

Bowles was actually born in Maryland in 1763 into a wealthy, Loyalist family. He enlisted in the British Army in 1778 at the age of 15. The regiment was transferred to Pensacola later that year. Bowles disliked the discipline of the army and deserted. He was accepted by Creeks living outside of Pensacola. There, he acquired the Indian name Estajoca and two Indian wives.

When the Spanish attacked the British at Pensacola in 1781 during the Revolutionary War, Bowles reappeared as the leader of a group of Indians who came to aid the British. During the late 1780s, he was simply a smuggler, trying to carry on trade with the Indians without attracting the attention of the U.S. or Spain.

In 1783, the Treaty of Paris, which ended the American Revolution, transferred the territory the Creeks were living in from Britain to Spain. This angered many of the Creeks because they felt their land had been traded without their permission. Bowles and several Indian leaders went to England to plead their case. The British refused to help.

Bowles returned to Florida in 1799 and proclaimed himself Director General of the Creek Nation. He declared the Creek and Seminole land in the middle of Florida as the State of Muscogee. Its capital was the Indian town of Miccosuckee, about 20 miles northeast of Tallahassee.

Bowles again asked the British for help, and offered that the State of Muscogee might become an important British ally. This concerned both the Spanish and the U.S., neither of whom wanted the British to regain a foothold in the region. Spain organized an attack on Miccosuckee in 1801, but failed to gain control.

The U.S. sent Benjamin Hawkins, a respected Indian negotiator and diplomat, to meet Bowles at a conference in Alabama, which was then part of Florida. When Bowles showed up, Hawkins arrested him and turned him over to the Spanish. Bowles was imprisoned in Havana, Cuba, until his death in 1805. Over the next 100 years, several important Seminole leaders took the name "Billy Bowlegs" as a tribute to him.

Many settlers began talking about independence or annexation by the United States. In West Florida, where Spanish control was weakest, settlers captured Baton Rouge in the fall of 1810 and proclaimed the establishment of the Republic of West Florida. They immediately called for the United States to annex the region, which it did, moving troops in to occupy it.

In 1811, General George Matthews of Georgia invaded Florida with a "patriot army" of 70 men. Outside of Saint Augustine he deployed cannon, but they were no match for the thick walls of Saint Augustine and Castillo de San Marcos. Spanish forces easily drove the Americans from Florida. Many of Matthews's troops were killed as they retreated into Georgia.

In 1814, the British entered Florida once again. Admiral Cochran of the British Navy landed near the mouth of the Apalachicola River and constructed a wooden fort. He supplied local Seminole Indians and former slaves with weapons and paid them to raid U.S. territories to the north. The United States asked Spain to remove the British and their "Negro Fort," but the Spanish refused to act.

Spain's inability to control its colony was becoming increasingly worrisome to the United States. In 1817, a large group of Seminole gathered near present-day Tallahassee. Word spread to the Spanish and the Americans that the Seminole were planning attacks in Georgia and farther north.

Seminole warriors are held captive by U.S. soldiers under the command of General Andrew Jackson in the First Seminole War in 1820.

U.S. TERRITORY

Less than a year later, in 1818, the United States sent a force of nearly 1,000 men under the command of Andrew Jackson to control the Seminole. Jackson was a veteran of the War of 1812, liked by his men, and known for his bravery and toughness. Shortly after reaching Florida, Jackson wrote to the new U.S. president, James Monroe, offering to take complete control of Florida. Jackson said, *"Let it be signified to me through any channel that the possession of the Floridas would be desirable to the United States, and in sixty days it will be accomplished."*

Jackson attacked a large Seminole town near Tallahassee in what became known as the First Seminole War. Many of the Seminole fled west to the frontier or south into the Everglades.

Jackson's men also captured two British men near the Seminole town. He believed that the two men, Alexander Arbuthnot and Robert Ambrister, were helping the Seminole. He gave each a quick military trial and sentenced each to death. Jackson later wrote, *"My God would not have smiled on me, had I punished only the poor ignorant savages, and spared the white men who set them on."*

Jackson next claimed to have found proof that the Spanish had encouraged and supported the Seminole gathering. He marched on the rebuilt fort at San Marcos de Apalachee and destroyed it. Then he attacked and occupied Pensacola.

The Spanish wrote to Washington D.C., demanding that Jackson be removed and punished. The U.S. secretary of state, John Quincy Adams, refused to do either. Adams suggested that Spain had two choices: *"either place a force in Florida adequate at once to the protection of her territory, . . . or cede [it] to the United States."* Finally Spain decided it was better to negotiate with the United States and give up its claim to Florida than to invest more money and troops there.

In February 1819, Luis de Onis, foreign minister of Spain, came to Washington to meet with Adams and work out the details of the agreement. On February 22, they concluded the Adams-Onis Treaty. Under the treaty, Florida became a territory of the United States. ✳

After Florida was returned to Spain at the end of the American Revolutionary War, growing American concern over possible interference with trade on the Mississippi, the desire for more plantation land, and a request by the people of the Republic of West Florida to be made part of the United States led to the gradual U.S. take over of the region. In 1795, Spain gave up its claims to the lands lying north of the 1763 Proclamation Line (see map page 78). In 1810, following a settlers' revolt, the United States annexed the area between the Mississippi and Pearl Rivers. In 1812, this region was added to the new state of Louisiana. The rest of Florida did not officially become U.S. territory until the Adams-Onis Treaty was signed with Spain in 1821.

TIME LINE

1513 Juan Ponce de León claims Florida for Spain.

1521 Juan Ponce de León returns to Florida but is attacked by the Calusa Indians and killed.

1527 Pánfilo de Narváez departs Spain to establish a colony in Florida. The mission is a failure.

1539 Hernando de Soto lands near present-day Tampa Bay with more than 1,000 men.

1549 Fr. Luis Cancer de Barbastro begins missionary work among the Indians of Florida, who kill him.

1559 Tristán de Luna attempts to establish a colony near present-day Pensacola. A hurricane destroys much of his food and supplies.

1562 Jean Ribault claims land near present-day Jacksonville for France.

1564 René de Laudonnière establishes a French colony called Fort Caroline.

1565 Pedro Menéndez de Avilés is sent by Spain to remove the French from Florida. Menéndez establishes Saint Augustine.

1585 Sir Francis Drake bombards Saint Augustine.

1577 Franciscan missionaries begin work in Florida.

1593 There are more than 20 missions in Florida, extending up the Atlantic coast into present-day Georgia and west cross Florida's central and panhandle regions.

1633 Missions reach the Apalachee in central Florida.

1660 The English begin working to establish the Carolina colony, north of Spanish Florida.

1668 Robert Searles, an English pirate, attacks and burns Saint Augustine to the ground.

1672 Construction begins on Castillo de San Marcos, a stone fort at Saint Augustine.

1682 La Salle, a Frenchman, locates the mouth of the Mississippi River on the Gulf of Mexico.

1698 Spanish forces build a fort at Pensacola.

1702 Colonel James Moore attacks Saint Augustine. After 50 days of siege, Spanish ships arrive to reinforce Saint Augustine, and Moore is forced to retreat.

1703 Moore attacks the missions, burning them to the ground, and kills or enslaves Indians who have been living there.

1713 Fewer than 400 Indians remain in the mission system.

1715 The Yamassee War breaks out in Carolina.

1732 Britain establishes the Georgia colony in the "debatable land" between Carolina and Florida.

1738 Villa Gracia Real Santa Teresa de Mose is established by the Spanish, two miles north of Saint Augustine.

1738 The War of Jenkins's Ear, between Spain and Britain, begins.

1739 James Oglethorpe, governor of Georgia, attacks Saint Augustine and the Castillo de San Marcos.

1750 Creek, Yamassee, and Apalachee Indians flee south into Florida and form the Indian group that will become known as Seminoles.

1763 As part of the Treaty of Paris that ends the French and Indian War, Spain is forced to give Florida to the British.

1766 Andrew Turnbull establishes New Smyrna and delivers more than 1,500 settlers to Florida.

1776 The 13 Colonies declare themselves independent from British rule. Florida remains loyal to Britain.

1777 American forces prepare to attack the British at Saint Augustine but are turned back before reaching the city.

1781 Spanish forces support Americans by attacking British troops at Pensacola.

1783 The American Revolution ends; Britain returns Florida to the Spanish.

1804 More than 750 European settlers apply for land grants in Florida.

1811 General George Matthews attacks the British at Saint Augustine but is defeated.

1818 U.S. forces under Andrew Jackson attack Seminole forces in central Florida.

1819 Under the Adams-Onis Treaty, the U.S. agrees to purchase East Florida from Spain.

1821 Spain and the U.S. sign the Adams-Onis Treaty, making Florida a U.S. territory.

RESOURCES

BOOKS

Castillo de San Marcos: A Guide to Castillo de San Marcos National Monument, Florida. Interior Department, National Park Service Division of Publications, 1994.

* Gannon, Michael. *Florida: A Short History.* Florida: University of Florida Press, 1993.

Hinshaw-Patent, Dorothy. *Treasures of the Spanish Main.* New York: Benchmark Press, 1999.

Sansevere-Dreher, Diane. *Explorers Who Got Lost.* New York: Tor Books, 2005.

Slavicek, Louise Chipley. *Juan Ponce De León (The Great Hispanic Heritage Series).* New York: Chelsea House Publications, 2003.

Thompson, William. *The Spanish Exploration of Florida: The Adventure of Spanish Conquistadors, incuding Juan Ponce De León, Pánfilo de Narváez, Álvar Núñez Cabeza De Vaca, Hernando De Soto, and Pedro Menéndez de Avilés in the American South.* Pennsylvania: Mason Crest Publishers, 2002.

* college-level source

WEB SITES

Florida Kids
http://dhr.dos.state.fl.us/kids/
Hosted by the state of Florida's Office for Cultural and Historical Programs, this page covers history and state facts just for kids.

The Library of Congress Presents America's Story from America's Library: Explore the States Florida
http://www.americaslibrary.gov/cgi-bin/page.cgi/es/fl
Part of the Library of Congress Web page for children, the Florida page links many Florida resource and articles as well as links to information about other states.

Florida Memory Project
http://www.floridamemory.com/
Hosted by the State Library and Archives of Florida, this page provides a searchable database of pictures and media files, spanning three hundred years of Florida history.

Spanish Colonial St. Augustine: A Resource for Teachers
http://web.uflib.ufl.edu/digital/collections/Teachers/index.htm
A collection of letters, notes and exhibits about colonial Saint Augustine.

Castillo de San Marcos National Monument
http://www.nps.gov/casa/home/home.htm
This page houses a series of articles about the Castillo de San Marcos written for students. It also contains information about visiting the fort.

Exploring Florida
http://fcit.usf.edu/florida/default.htm
This site includes social studies resources for students and teachers and includes in-depth coverage of explorers and images of the reconstructed mission at San Luis de Apalachee.

QUOTE SOURCES

CHAPTER ONE

p. 15 "De León...with them."
Fulson, Robert H. *Juan Ponce De León and the Spanish Discovery of Puerto Rico and Florida*. Virginia: McDonald & Woodward Publishing Company, 2000, p. 114; "Among the...young again." McNutt, Francis A. De Orbe Novo, *The Eight Decades of Peter Martyr d Anghera*. New York: G.P Putman, 1912, p.274; p. 17 "I discovered...with (other) lands." Van Middeldyk, R.A., editor, Brumbaugh, Martin G. *The History of Puerto Rico, from the Spanish Discovery to the American Occupation*. New York: D. Appleton and Company, 1903, p. 75; p. 19 "It seemed to... adapted to settlement." http://www.floridahistory.com/cab-text.html, paragraph 16.

CHAPTER TWO

p. 26 "one of...of the world." http://memory.loc.gov/cgi-bin/query/r?intldl/ascfr:@field(DOCID+@lit(gcfr0018_0177); p. 33 "I do this...Lutherans." http://digital.library.upenn.edu/women/marshall/country/country-I-9.html. Marshall, Henrietta Elizabeth, *This Country of Ours: the Story of the United States*. New York: Goerge H. Doran Company, 1917, Chapter 9, paragraph 43; p.35 "Shall we....Was I wrong?" http://digital.library.upenn.edu/women/marshall/country/country-I-10.html. Marshall, chapter 10, paragraph 2; p. 36 "I do this...Murderers." http://digital.library.upenn.edu/women/marshall/country/country-I-10.html. Marshall, chapter 10, paragraph 25.

CHAPTER THREE

p.39 "our principal intent... Catholic Faith." Gannon, Michael. *The New History of Florida*. Gainesville, FL: University of Florida Press, 1996, p. 78; p.44 "they are...men alike." Gannon, p. 82; p. 49 "It became...other services." http://www.flheritage.com/archaeology/sanluis/facts/vol5.cfm, paragraph 3; "Each year...them a wage." http://www.flheritage.com/archaeology/sanluis/facts/vol5.cfm, paragraph 2; p. 50 "There are ...and other trifles." http://www.flheritage.com/archaeology/sanluis/facts/vol5.cfm, paragraphs 1–3, 6.

CHAPTER FOUR

p. 55 "give way...in cheese." http://www.cr.nps.gov/history/online books/source/is1/is1d.htm, paragraph 15; p. 58 "the best bay I have ever seen in my life." Gannon, Michael, *The New History of Florida*. Gainesville, FL: University of Florida Press, 1996, p. 118; pp. 59–60 "I built the ...French squadron saw it." Gannon, p. 120.

CHAPTER SIX

p. 79 "a struggling...with weeds." Coker, William S., et al. *Florida: From the Beginning to 1992*. Houston, TX : Pioneer Publications, 1991, chapter 8, p.1; p. 81 "the most... American dominions." Coker, chapter 8, p. 1; p. 85 "There is... dancing mad." Coker, chapter 8, p. 4.

CHAPTER EIGHT

p. 96 "Our vessels...good market here." From the Collections of William and Sue Goza and Thomas and Georgine Mickler, University of Florida Libraries, Special and Area Collections, P. K. Yonge Library of Florida History. *Extract of a letter from a gentleman in St. Augustine, Jan. 12, saying Gov. Zespedes of Spanish East Florida is cordial and welcoming to merchants*; p. 102 "Let it...be accomplished." Remini, Robert V. *The Life of Andrew Jackson*. New York: Harper & Row Publishers Inc. 1988. p 118; "My God...set them on." www.andrewjackson.org, paragraph 34; pp. 102–103 "either place...United States." Gannon, Michael, *The New History of Florida*. Gainesville, FL: University of Florida Press, 1996, chapter 12, p. 207.

INDEX

ABOUT THE AUTHOR AND CONSULTANT

MATTHEW C. CANNAVALE has written and edited numerous books for middle-grade readers, including several biographies and historical accounts about milestones in science. He has undergraduate degrees in English and secondary education and earned a graduate degree from the Harvard Graduate School of Education. He currently lives in Brighton, Massachusetts.

ROBERT OLWELL is an Associate Professor of History at the University of Texas at Austin. He is the author or editor of several books, including *Master's, Slaves, and Subjects: The Culture of Power in the South Carolina Low Country, 1740–1790* and *Cultures and Identities in Colonial British America* as well as numerous articles on the subject of American colonial history. He has graduate degrees from the University of Wisconsin-Milwaukee and the Johns Hopkins University and lives in Austin, Texas.

ILLUSTRATION CREDITS

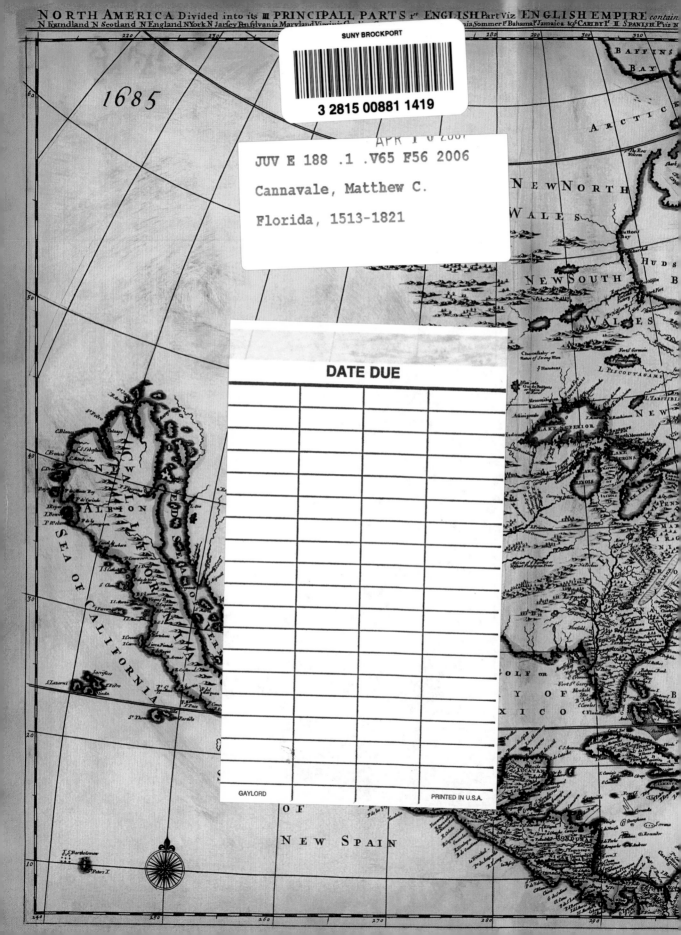

DATE DUE